Weaving It Together

FOURTH EDITION

CONNECTING **READING** AND **WRITING**

NATIONAL GEOGRAPHIC LEARNING

CENGAGE Learning

Australia • Brazil • Japan • Korea • Mexico • Singapore • Spain • United Kingdom • United States

Teacher's Guide Books 1 and 2: Weaving It Together: Connecting Reading and Writing, Fourth Edition

Milada Broukal

Publisher: Sherrise Roehr

Executive Editor: Laura Le Dréan

Acquisitions Editor: Jennifer Monaghan

Contributing Editor: Bernard Seal

Director of Global Marketing: Ian Martin

Executive Product Marketing Manager:
Benjamin D. Rivera

Product Marketing Manager:
Anders Bylund

Sr. Director, ELT & World Languages:
Michael Burggren

Production Manager: Daisy Sosa

Content Project Manager:
Andrea Bobotas

Print Buyer: Mary Beth Hennebury

Cover Designer: Michael Rosenquest

Cover Image: Landsat 7 ETM+ image,
©NASA/USGS, processed by Serge
Andréfouët, University of South
Florida/Institut de Recherche pour le
Développement

Text Design and Layout: Don Williams

Composition: Page Designs International

For product information and technology assistance, contact us at
Cengage Learning Customer & Sales Support,
1-800-354-9706

For permission to use material from this text or product,
submit all requests online at **www.cengage.com/permissions**.
Further permissions questions can be e-mailed to
permissionrequest@cengage.com.

Teacher's Guide ISBN: 978-1-305-25172-4

National Geographic Learning
20 Channel Center Street
Boston, MA 02210
USA

Cengage Learning is a leading provider of customized learning solutions with office locations around the globe, including Singapore, the United Kingdom, Australia, Mexico, Brazil, and Japan.

Cengage Learning products are represented in Canada by Nelson Education, Ltd.

Visit National Geographic Learning online at **NGL.cengage.com**.

Visit our corporate website at **www.cengage.com**.

Printed in the United States of America
Print Number: 01   Print Year: 2015

Contents

Introduction

OVERALL OBJECTIVES OF THE SERIES

Weaving It Together, *Books 1 and 2* are the first two books in a four-level series that integrates reading and writing for students of English as a second or foreign language. The central premise of *Weaving It Together* is that reading and writing are interwoven and inextricable skills. Good readers write well; good writers read well. With this premise in mind, *Weaving It Together* has been developed to meet the following objectives:

- To combine reading and writing through a comprehensive, systematic, and engaging process designed to integrate the two effectively.
- To provide academically bound students with serious and engaging multicultural content.
- To promote individualized and cooperative learning within medium- to large-sized classes.

ORGANIZATION OF THE STUDENT BOOKS

Each level of *Weaving It Together* contains eight thematically organized units with two related readings in each unit. The themes have been carefully selected to appeal to a wide range of interests and to promote discussion and comparison of different cultures. The readings provide input intended to generate a variety of responses, and students should be encouraged to ask further questions about the readings and to question their own and each other's opinions in an open and constructive way. These ideas are later expanded through vocabulary, reading comprehension, discussion, and critical thinking activities, and lead to writing tasks that grow naturally out of the previous reading and discussion.

Each unit ends with a final series of three optional activities that include having students write under time pressure, do Internet research, and answer some questions about the two readings in the unit.

UNIT STRUCTURE

The following sequence of activities occurs twice in each unit of *Weaving It Together*, *Books 1 and 2*:

READING
- Pre-reading
    - Preparing for the Reading Topic
    - Key Vocabulary
- Reading Passage
- Vocabulary
    - Vocabulary in Context
    - Vocabulary Building
- Reading Comprehension
    - Looking for Main Ideas
    - Looking for Details
- Discussion
- Critical Thinking

WRITING
- Writing Skills
    - Exercises
- Writing Practice
    - Pre-writing
    - Revising and Editing
    - Writing Final Copy

Each step in the sequence is important to the final goal of enabling students to produce excellent written English. The skills of reading, writing, generating ideas, and developing vocabulary are integrated throughout each chapter, with the aim of achieving this goal. (See the sample lesson plan on pages 5–7 for suggestions on timing and how to use each stage of the lesson.)

GRADING OF WRITTEN WORK

The process of rewriting and editing written work is consistently emphasized in this series. Encourage your students to hand in at least one preliminary draft of their work before handing in their final draft. As you evaluate student work, be sure to value original and thoughtful writing, as well as the amount of effort invested in the work.

Here are some suggestions for correcting students' written work:

- Use editing symbols so that students have to find their own mistakes (see page 8). You may want to provide students with a list of these symbols so that they can refer to them when looking at your corrections of their work. An example of how you might mark up an essay using these symbols is given on page 9.

- Explain to students your criteria for grading written work. You may want to use the same criteria each time, or you may prefer to focus on specific points. You might focus on paragraph formatting for the first assignment, for example, and then gradually add other evaluative criteria, such as grammar, vocabulary, and content. See page 10 for a sample grading rubric, which may be adapted for your class.

- Have students work in pairs to check their written work before handing it in. Peer editing is a great way to help students learn to become more independent writers. Encourage students to use the Paragraph Checklist in the Writing Practice sections when correcting each other's work.

- Try to limit the number of corrections you make by focusing only on errors that impede meaning or only on the grammar or organizational points taught in the Writing Skills sections. If one mistake recurs frequently in a student's writing, correct it just once and ask the student to find other examples of the mistake by himself or herself.

- Remember to use a balance of both praise and criticism in your comments.

JOURNALS

Journals, although they are optional in the *Weaving It Together* series, provide an effective way of increasing the value of class time, as they encourage learning outside of class. Students can experiment with new words or phrases they have recently learned, prepare their thoughts about a topic before discussing it in class, or respond in a personal way to the topics of class discussions. Journals are especially effective with shy or quiet students, who may not feel comfortable speaking out in class. They are also an excellent way for you to get direct feedback from students as to how well they have understood a lesson and what their feelings are about the topics under discussion. Journals can provide direct communication with individual students on a regular basis.

Not all students will find it easy to write a journal. Some may not be used to this type of writing; others may wish to have every word corrected by the teacher. It is important to explain your goals and the purpose of the journal in your course.

You can use journals in many different ways, including the following:

- Suggest that students keep a journal in their free time, as a way of gathering ideas for their writing assignments. They don't have to hand it in or have it corrected, or they may have the option to do so.

- Use journals for free writing, and have students hand them in a certain number of times during the semester. Respond with encouraging comments or reactions, but do not correct spelling, grammar, or other errors.

- Use journals to interact with your students in an ongoing written dialogue about topics you have discussed in class or about their learning progress. Again, this writing probably will not be corrected or graded in any way.

- Ask students to choose a journal writing partner, with whom they can exchange journals. This allows more independence from the teacher. Partners should write comments on each other's work (but be sure to give students guidelines as to how to comment and what to comment on).

- Use the journal as a graded component of the course, grading only effort and participation, not language accuracy.

Using journals in your class will create extra work for you. However, the more enthusiastic you are about journals, the better your students will respond, and you may find yourself learning a great deal that will ultimately help you to understand your students better and aid you in your classroom teaching. Suggestions for journal writing tasks are given throughout this manual.

INTERNET ACTIVITY

At the end of each unit is an activity called Search the Internet. This activity can be done in a classroom setting with the guidance of the teacher or as a homework task leading to a classroom presentation or discussion. At first, students may find searching the Internet in English difficult. Give advice on how to search and encourage students to share tips. We have not suggested any specific Web sites, as URLs change frequently, but suggestions are provided in the Student Books and in this manual of keywords that can be used with a search engine.

Remember that not all Web sites provide accurate information. Students should be advised to compare several sites to help verify data. Be careful to warn students of the dangers of providing any personal information to Web sites or downloading any files from unknown sources.

We hope that you and your students will enjoy using the *Weaving It Together* series!

Sample Lesson Plan

Weaving It Together follows a carefully designed sequence of activities, which guides students through the process of connecting reading to writing. Allow approximately 6 to 8 hours of class time for each unit. Remember that each of the sample lessons below will be done twice since there are two readings and two extended writing activities in each unit. The following time allotments are suggestions only.

LESSON 1 (100 MINUTES)

UNIT PHOTO AND WARM-UP (10 MINUTES)

The unit opens with an impactful photo that reflects the theme of the unit. Use the photo to ask students questions related to the general theme and to gather ideas to be used later in their writing. The unit opener also contains the What Do You Think? activity, which taps students' background knowledge and generates interest in the topic of the readings in the unit. Have students answer the What Do You Think? activity individually. When they have finished, match students with a partner and have them compare their answers.

PREPARING FOR THE READING TOPIC (10 MINUTES)

Use the photos accompanying the reading and the Preparing for the Reading Topic questions to introduce the specific theme of the chapter. Activating students' background knowledge of the topic will make the readings easier to understand.

KEY VOCABULARY (10 MINUTES)

The Key Vocabulary activity introduces the vocabulary highlighted in the reading. This exercise may be done before the reading, in order to make the reading easier, or after the reading, as a review. Note that the vocabulary in the exercise is in the order that it appears in the reading, making it easier for the students to find the vocabulary.

VOCABULARY AND READING COMPREHENSION (45 MINUTES)

To encourage effective reading skills, you may wish to follow this procedure:

- Ask students two or three easy comprehension questions that will guide them to the main points of the reading. Set a time limit of about 3 minutes for students to find the answers quickly.

- Have students read the general comprehension questions (Looking for Main Ideas), and then set a time limit of 5 to 8 minutes for a second reading of the passage. Then give students 10 minutes to write their answers or to discuss them in pairs. Have students check the answers by referring back to the passage.

- Have students answer the Vocabulary in Context questions, which helps them develop an in-depth understanding of the eight target words in the reading that have been chosen for them to study.

- There may be other words in the reading that students may be unfamiliar with. Give them a chance to search for and guess the meanings of any unknown words. Then have students answer the detailed comprehension questions (Looking for Details), referring back to the reading for the answers.

- Use the teaching hints in this Teacher's Guide for additional ideas on using the reading and extending the comprehension activities.

DISCUSSION AND CRITICAL THINKING QUESTIONS (25 MINUTES)

The Discussion and Critical Thinking questions give students a chance to respond to the readings on a personal level by relating the theme to their own concerns and giving their personal opinions. The result is a deeper processing of the material, which will help students remember the vocabulary and the theme and develop ideas to use in their writing later.

LESSON 2 (100 MINUTES)

REVIEW (10 MINUTES)

Review the vocabulary and themes from the first lesson. Extend the vocabulary to include words and phrases related to students' own cultural context, if appropriate. Encourage students to keep a systematic record of the new vocabulary they are learning in a notebook or on cards, adding definitions and example sentences to help them remember the words.

WRITING SKILLS (40 MINUTES)

Present the new grammar or organizational writing point to be practiced in this lesson. Make sure that students understand these points well since they will be called upon to use this newly acquired knowledge to do the exercises that follow and in the Writing Practice section. Allow students plenty of time to complete all tasks. Have students compare their answers when appropriate.

WRITING PRACTICE (50 MINUTES)

Pre-Writing. In Level 1, students write sentences in answer to questions. They will use these answers later to write a paragraph. In Level 2, students do a variety of pre-writing activities before they write a rough draft of a paragraph. In either case, go over the questions and the tasks as a class, making sure that students clearly understand the questions and the nature of their pre-writing task. As students write their answers or do their pre-writing task, walk around the class to answer questions and monitor students' work. Make sure students reread their work carefully before going on to the next task.

Writing. In Level 1, students will use the sentences they wrote in the first activity to construct a paragraph. For the first chapters of the book, you might want to write a model on the board, showing the differences between writing sentences and writing a paragraph, both in layout and in the use of pronouns. They use a paragraph checklist to check that they have appropriately constructed their paragraph and then work together in pairs to edit their paragraphs and check for accuracy. Finally, they write a clean "final copy" of their paragraph. In Level 2, students follow a similar set of steps once they have done their pre-writing tasks.

OPTIONAL LESSON (100 MINUTES)

The *Weaving It Together* last page of each unit is optional. It contains three activities and teachers may decide to do all three, two, one, or none of the activities.

TIMED WRITING (65 MINUTES)

In Levels 1 and 2, students write answers to a series of questions before writing a paragraph under timed conditions. Students are given 50 minutes to write. Before they start writing, however, quickly review for them what they have learned about how to write effective paragraphs.

SEARCH THE INTERNET (30 MINUTES)

One of the aims of Internet activities is to provide students with an opportunity to develop the skills needed for independent study. These tasks, therefore, are designed for students to complete on their own time, bringing the results of their research to class for discussion. You therefore will want to assign the Internet activity as homework. The first few times you assign this activity for homework, give students tips on how to search for information online. If you are able to connect to the Internet in class and project a computer screen, demonstrate search techniques or have students demonstrate them.

WHAT DO YOU THINK NOW? (5 MINUTES)

This activity provides an opportunity for final discussion of the topic and the readings covered. Have students answer the activity individually *without* referring to the readings. Check the answers as a class, looking back at the readings if necessary.

Editing Symbols

The following symbols may be used or adapted for marking up students' written work. By placing the symbol next to or above the error, students can try to work out where the problem is and self-correct.

Symbol	Explanation
cap	Capital letter
lc	Lowercase (word or words incorrectly capitalized)
p	Punctuation incorrect or missing
sp	Spelling mistake
sv	Mistake in agreement of subject and verb
∧	Omission (something has been left out)
frag	Sentence fragment (correct by completing sentence)
ro	Run-on sentence (insert period and capital letter or add comma and conjunction)
vt	Incorrect verb tense
vf	Verb incorrectly formed
modal	Incorrect use or formation of modal
cond	Incorrect use or formation of a conditional sentence
ss	Incorrect sentence structure
wo	Incorrect or awkward word order
conn	Incorrect or missing connector
pass	Incorrect formation or use of passive voice
unclear	Unclear message
art	Incorrect or missing article
num	Problem with the singular or plural of a noun
wc	Wrong word choice, including prepositions
wf	Wrong word form
nonidiom	Nonidiomatic (not expressed this way in English)
coh	Coherence; one idea does not lead to the next
pro re	Pronoun reference unclear or incorrect
pro agree	Pronoun agreement unclear or incorrect
trans	Incorrect transition or transition needed
¶	Begin a new paragraph here (indent)

Sample Edited Essay

The following essay shows how a student essay might be marked up using the Editing Symbols on page 8.

Comparing Living in a City with Living in a Small Town

Our life is affected extremely by environmental conditions such as people, friends, and jobs. Finding good place to live is one important   *art*

sv   thing that have an effect on our life. There are many different

wc   opinions between living in a big city and living in a small town.

A big city and a small town are both places to live.

lc   Another Way a big city is like a small town is they have houses,   *pro re*

transportation, trees, and people. In addition, a big city and a small

town both have restaurants, entertainment places, and park for   *num*

people to enjoy after work.

p   However there are some differences between living in a big

city and a small town. The economic in a big city is better than   *wf*

ss   in a small town. A big city, It has companies and factories more

cap   than a small city. moreover, the population of a big city are too   *sv*

overcrowded. Because most overpopulation problems are from the   *frag*

sv   big cities. In a small town, people seems to be more friendly than

ro   in a big city, they know each other and treat there neighbors like   *sp*

vt   family. There were less violence in a small town. People like to live

wf   in a peace world rather than to compete with others. On the other

hand, living in a big city is more funny than a small town.   *wc*

In brief, living place is very important to people. Chosing a   *sp*

modal   wrong place to live could be badly affect people's life, especially for

conn   their children. Nevertheless, whether it is a big city or small town, it

is necessary to observe all the things surrounding us.

Grading Rubric

The following rubric may be used or adapted for grading your students' written work. Assign a grade of 1 to 5 for each item (1 = inadequate, 5 = excellent). Then give students an average grade from 1 to 5 for each category, Content, Organization, etc.

1. Content

a. Clear development of main idea or thesis   1   2   3   4   5

b. Sufficient and relevant supporting details   1   2   3   4   5

c. Original thinking about the topic   1   2   3   4   5

Average _____

2. Organization

a. Correct organization of ideas within the essay or paragraph   1   2   3   4   5

b. Logical sequence of ideas   1   2   3   4   5

c. Main points and supporting details clearly expressed   1   2   3   4   5

Average _____

3. Vocabulary

a. Good range of vocabulary for this level   1   2   3   4   5

b. Appropriate choice of words for this level   1   2   3   4   5

Average _____

4. Language use

a. Correct use of grammar structures for this level   1   2   3   4   5

b. Correct use of articles, nouns, and prepositions   1   2   3   4   5

c. Correct use of cohesive devices such as pronouns and transition words   1   2   3   4   5

Average _____

5. Mechanics

a. Correct spelling and use of punctuation and capitalization   1   2   3   4   5

b. Correct use of paragraph format   1   2   3   4   5

c. Good presentation (paper is neatly prepared)   1   2   3   4   5

Average _____

LEVEL 1

Teaching Hints
and Answer Key

Special Days

In this opening unit of the book, students read about a special holiday in India and about birthday celebrations around the world. The topics of special holidays and birthdays will give the students opportunities to talk about their personal lives and thus build class rapport. They will talk about what special days they particularly enjoy in their cultures and how they celebrate birthdays. Use the unit opener photo to brainstorm different holidays.

READING ▪ 1
A Festival of Colors

PRE-READING   page 4

Begin the lesson in one of the following ways:

- Although this reading is not about New Year's Eve, discussing New Year's celebrations around the world is a good way to get into the topic of special days. Tell students about how Americans celebrate New Year's Eve in New York City's Times Square by watching a huge crystal ball drop from a tall building and how people around the country watch this on television. Then at midnight, people hug and kiss and sing "Auld Lang Syne." Now have students give details about New Year's Eve in their countries and cultures.

- Have students write their favorite holiday on the back of a card. Collect all the cards and then redistribute them. Students walk around the room and try to find the person who wrote a particular holiday on the back of the card: "Is your favorite holiday *X*?" When they find the person who wrote the name of the holiday, they then ask questions about what happens on that day.

- Look at the title of the reading and the reading opener photo and try to tease apart with the class the difference in meaning between a "festival" and a "holiday."

PREPARING FOR THE READING TOPIC
Answers will vary.

KEY VOCABULARY

1. d	**3.** f	**5.** a	**7.** c
2. h	**4.** e	**6.** g	**8.** b

VOCABULARY   pages 6–7
VOCABULARY IN CONTEXT

A
1. relax	**5.** celebrate
2. powders	**6.** throw
3. equal	**7.** have fun
4. all over	**8.** festival

B *Answers will vary.*

VOCABULARY BUILDING

1. all over the world
2. all over my clothes
3. celebrate the New Year
4. celebrate my birthday

READING COMPREHENSION pages 7–8

LOOKING FOR MAIN IDEAS

Possible answers:

1. The festival of Holi celebrates the beginning of spring and also how good is stronger than evil.

2. On the night before Holi, the men and boys make a big fire and families sing and dance around the fire.

3. Holi is called the *Festival of Colors* because people throw colored powders and water on one another. Afterward, everyone looks like a walking rainbow.

LOOKING FOR DETAILS

1. F		**3.** T		**5.** F	
2. T		**4.** F		**6.** F	

Additional Reading Activity

Ask the students to read the reading passage again and to create a timeline of the different things that happen before Holi and at different times during the day and evening of the Holi festival. Show students how to make a timeline by drawing a line on the board. Ask students to tell you what points to include in the timeline: the days before Holi, the night before Holi, the morning of Holi, etc.

DISCUSSION page 8

Answers will vary.

CRITICAL THINKING page 8

Answers will vary.

WRITING ■ 1

WRITING SKILLS pages 9–12

EXERCISE 1

1. <u>The boys</u> make a fire.
2. <u>They</u> are happy.
3. <u>Our family</u> prepares special food.
4. <u>The Hindu woman</u> prepares special food.
5. <u>The Hindu woman with the white hair</u> prepares special food.
6. <u>The days of Holi</u> are fun.
7. <u>Rich people and poor people</u> are equal at this time.
8. <u>Young people and old people</u> have fun.

EXERCISE 2

1. People <u>close</u> the shops.
2. Hindus <u>are going to celebrate</u> Holi.
3. My family <u>celebrates</u> Holi.
4. Young and old people <u>have</u> fun.
5. Families <u>sing</u> and <u>dance</u> around the fire.
6. My family and other Hindu families in the United States <u>celebrate</u> Holi.
7. The men and the boys <u>make</u> a big fire.
8. Boys and girls <u>are dancing</u> around the fire.

EXERCISE 3

1. People wear <u>old clothes</u>.
2. People are celebrating <u>the Festival of Colors</u>.
3. The festival celebrates <u>the beginning of spring</u>.
4. People buy <u>powders of different colors</u>.
5. Women prepare <u>special foods for the festival</u>.
6. People enjoy <u>this time</u>.

7. They also throw <u>colored water</u>.

8. They wash their <u>faces, bodies, and clothes</u>.

EXERCISE 4

1. The festival is in **F**ebruary.

2. **I**to and **M**ayumi are from **T**okyo, **J**apan.

3. **T**he American woman celebrated **C**hinese **N**ew **Y**ear with us.

4. **I**n our class, we have students who are **B**uddhist, **M**uslim, **C**hristian, and **J**ewish.

5. **M**aria is from **M**exico **C**ity, **M**exico.

6. **M**y mother and **I** were born in **A**ugust.

7. **I** am going to be in **N**ew **Y**ork on **N**ew **Y**ear's **D**ay.

8. **M**r. **J**ones and I are going to a party on **F**riday.

EXERCISE 5

Jim and Barbara Miller live in **C**hicago, in the **U**nited **S**tates. They are **A**mericans. Jim is **C**hristian and **B**arbara is Buddhist. They **celebrate** **T**hanksgiving in **N**ovember. It **is** an important holiday.

Additional Writing Skills Activity

Have students make lists headed: Cities, Countries, Languages, Special Days, Days of the Week, and Months of the Year. Ask them to write four examples of each that are different from the ones on page 11. Walk around the room, helping with spelling and checking to see that students used capital letters correctly.

WRITING PRACTICE pages 12–13

Answers vary throughout this section.

Ask students to write about how they celebrate New Year's Eve and/or New Year's Day. Prompt them to write about what they eat, wear, and do.

READING ▪ 2
Birthdays around the World

PRE-READING page 14

Begin the lesson in one of the following ways:

- Write the word "birthdays" on the board and create a cluster diagram as students brainstorm words connected with this topic.

- Bring a gift-wrapped package into the classroom and talk with students about when people give and receive gifts. What do people say when they give and receive gifts?

- Ask students to line up in order from January to December according to when their birthday is. Make sure students know the names of the months of the year in English and how to answer the question: "What day is your birthday?" Students may not feel comfortable saying the year of their birth, so make sure that students are aware that they do not have to say this in order to do this activity.

- Have students look at the photo in the reading opener and guess what is happening.

PREPARING FOR THE READING TOPIC
Answers will vary.

KEY VOCABULARY

1. e	**3.** h	**5.** b	**7.** c
2. d	**4.** a	**6.** g	**8.** f

VOCABULARY pages 17–18

VOCABULARY IN CONTEXT

A
1. customs
2. candles
3. gather around
4. breath

5. flag
6. flavors
7. lucky
8. decorate

B *Answers will vary.*

VOCABULARY BUILDING

1. lucky
2. luck
3. breath

4. breathe
5. flavors
6. flavor

READING COMPREHENSION pages 18–19

LOOKING FOR MAIN IDEAS

1. a   2. a   3. b

LOOKING FOR DETAILS

1. There is one candle for each year of your **life** on a birthday cake.

2. In Denmark, they put gifts around the child's **bed**.

3. Two **American** sisters wrote the famous birthday song.

4. In Holland, the **crown** years are 5, 10, 15, 20, and 21.

5. In Finland, the birthday child gets **breakfast** in bed.

6. In India, Hindu children celebrate their birthday **until** the age of 16.

Additional Reading Activity

Explain "scanning" to the class. Then have students scan the reading to find all the different countries that are mentioned. Have them circle the names of the countries in the reading or make a list. Give them a one- or two-minute time limit, depending on whether they are writing the names or circling the names. Have students compare their answers to see if they found them all. To help students, you could tell them that there are nine countries in the reading. The nine countries mentioned in the reading are the United States, Norway, Denmark, Sweden, Finland, Holland, Japan, India, and China.

DISCUSSION page 19

Answers will vary.

CRITICAL THINKING page 19

Answers will vary.

WRITING ▪ 2

WRITING SKILLS pages 20–21

EXERCISE 1

1. F   2. T   3. F   4. F   5. T

EXERCISE 2

My birthday is on **J**une 11. I was born in **L**ima, **P**eru. We **have** a party on my **b**irthday. My friends **come**. My mother make**s** a cake. I get many gift**s**. I **am** always happy on my birthday. It is my special **d**ay.

WRITING PRACTICE pages 21–22

Answers vary throughout this section.

Additional Writing Activity

Review the information on page 20 and have students write a short paragraph about what a paragraph is. They can title the paragraph: *The Paragraph*. For a low-level class, you will want to help them with the information that they can include and maybe even provide the first sentence: *A paragraph is a short piece of writing on one topic.*

JOURNAL

Ask students to write about birthday customs in their country or another culture that they know about.

WEAVING IT TOGETHER

TIMED WRITING page 23

Answers will vary.

SEARCH THE INTERNET page 23

A *Answers will vary.*

B Suggested keywords:
- birthday traditions around the world
- birthdays in Russia/Mexico/Thailand, etc.
- birthday songs
- birthday games

WHAT DO YOU THINK NOW? Page 23

1. celebrate
2. happy
3. are
4. eat

UNIT 2 Places

In this unit, students read about a famous city—Venice, and a country that they are unlikely to know much about—Iceland. During the study of this unit, students will get the opportunity to talk and write about places that they know and are familiar with. Use the unit opener photo to talk about good locations for a city.

READING ■ 1
Venice: A Changing City

PRE-READING page 26

Begin the lesson in one of the following ways:

- Bring into class some pictures of famous landmarks in famous cities: Times Square in New York City; Trafalgar Square or Buckingham Palace in London; the Eiffel Tower in Paris; the Sydney Opera House in Sydney, Australia; the Burj Khalifa in Dubai, etc. Put the pictures on the wall and number them. Have students write down all the numbers and walk around the room and write down the names of all the places and cities that they recognize next to the numbers. Check the answers as a class and have students ask questions about each place.

- With the class make a list of about ten countries on the board. Write down the name of the most famous city in each country. Then have students think of one adjective that describes each city. This task will help students with some of the writing tasks in the unit that ask students to use adjectives in describing cities.

- Have students look at the picture on pages 26–27. Find out how much they know about Venice.

PREPARING FOR THE READING TOPIC
Answers will vary.

KEY VOCABULARY

1. b	**3.** h	**5.** a	**7.** c
2. f	**4.** e	**6.** g	**8.** d

VOCABULARY pages 28–29
VOCABULARY IN CONTEXT

A
1. elderly	5. rent
2. unique	6. residents
3. bridges	7. alarm
4. romantic	8. boots

B *Answers will vary.*

VOCABULARY BUILDING

A
1. have fun
2. have a problem
3. have a meal

B *Answers will vary.*

READING COMPREHENSION pages 30–31
LOOKING FOR MAIN IDEAS

1. a   **2.** c   **3.** c

LOOKING FOR DETAILS

1. Venice is in the **north** of Italy.

2. People use **boats** to travel and bring things into Venice.

3. When there is a high tide, people walk on special **platforms**.

4. Today, Venice has **half** as many people as it had 30 years ago.

5. The old shops in Venice are changing to **souvenir** shops.

6. Residents are moving out of Venice because the houses are too **expensive**.

DISCUSSION   page 31

Answers will vary.

CRITICAL THINKING   page 31

Answers will vary.

WRITING ▪ 1

WRITING SKILLS   pages 32–33

EXERCISE 1

1. Venice is a <u>romantic</u> city.
2. There are <u>souvenir</u> shops everywhere.
3. The city has an <u>old</u> problem.
4. The houses are too <u>expensive</u>.
5. Venice is <u>beautiful</u>.

EXERCISE 2

1. Venice is a beautiful city.
2. Venice is in the north of Italy.
3. Venice is a group of 118 small islands.
4. Venice has a problem with high tide.

EXERCISE 3

Answers will vary.

EXERCISE 4

Venice is in the north of **I**taly. It is a **unique** city. Here you **don't** see roads with cars, but you see**s** **c**anals with boats. Everything in the city is expensive because everything comes by boat. Tourists **love** Venice. **O**ver 20 **m**illion tourist**s** come to visit Venice every year!

Additional Writing Skills Activity

Have students work in pairs. Have them look back at Reading 1 and find all the adjectives. Have them notice if the adjective comes before or after the noun that it describes. They should find: *beautiful* (before); *unique* (before); *new* (before); *special* (before); *beautiful, old, and romantic* (after); *good and bad* (after); *old* (before—three times); *high* (after); *old* (before); *expensive* (after); *rich* (before); *elderly* (before); *biggest* (before); *high* (before); *beautiful, old, and romantic* (before). Make sure students know which adjectives the nouns are modifying. This can be tricky for the adjectives that come after the noun.

WRITING PRACTICE   pages 33–34

Answers vary throughout this section.

JOURNAL

Ask students to describe a place that they have been to that they have enjoyed visiting. Have them write about why they found the place to be interesting and enjoyable. Ask them to use adjectives to describe the climate, the buildings, and the people.

READING ■ 2
Life Is Good in Iceland

PRE-READING   page 35

Begin the lesson in one of the following ways:

- Bring a map of the world into class. Have volunteers identify their own countries. Have other students ask about those countries: What languages are spoken there? How is the quality of life? Do people work hard? What is the health care system like? What is the weather like? Do people have to heat their homes or cool them? At what times of year? Is crime a problem?

- Have students think of five countries that are islands and five countries that do not border any ocean or sea.

- Have students look at the photo on page 36. Have them describe the picture and tell you why it seems unusual. Ask students what they think the temperature of the air is and what they think the temperature of the water might be. Do they have waters like these in their countries?

PREPARING FOR THE READING TOPIC

Answers will vary.

KEY VOCABULARY

1. c	**3.** h	**5.** b	**7.** f
2. a	**4.** g	**6.** e	**8.** d

VOCABULARY   pages 37–38

VOCABULARY IN CONTEXT

A
1. island
2. a quarter of
3. similar to
4. heat
5. crime
6. high quality of life
7. capital
8. temperature

B *Answers will vary.*

VOCABULARY BUILDING

1. air quality
2. quality of service
3. quality of life
4. quality of work

READING COMPREHENSION   pages 38–39

LOOKING FOR MAIN IDEAS

Possible answers:

1. Iceland is an island in the North Atlantic Ocean. It is between Greenland and Norway, but it is part of Europe.

2. Icelanders are the hardest workers in Europe.

3. Icelanders have a great system for health and education. Health care and education are free. All children must go to school from age 6 to age 16.

LOOKING FOR DETAILS

1. F	**3.** T	**5.** T
2. F	**4.** F	**6.** T

Additional Reading Activity

Ask each student to take a piece of paper and make two columns. Have them write "Positive" above one column and "Negative" above the other. Have students skim through the reading and list things that they think are positive and negative about Iceland. Explain that their answers will be subjective. For example, the reading says that students work hard in Iceland. For some students, this might be positive and others negative. Once they have compiled their lists, put students in pairs to compare their answers. Have students keep this piece of paper since it will help them answer the first question in the Critical Thinking section.

DISCUSSION page 39

Answers will vary.

CRITICAL THINKING page 39

Answers will vary.

WRITING ▪ 2

WRITING SKILLS pages 40–43

EXERCISE 1

1. 3; more beautiful than
2. 1; wetter than
3. 1; drier than
4. 3; more expensive than
5. 1; older than
6. 3; more dangerous than
7. 1; higher than
8. 1; larger than

EXERCISE 2

1. Iceland is bigger than Switzerland.
2. Iceland is smaller than Greenland.
3. The Pacific Ocean is larger than the Atlantic Ocean.
4. The Burj Tower in Dubai is taller than the Empire State Building in New York City.
5. The Nile River is longer than the Mississippi River.
6. Mexico is drier than Canada.
7. The Taj Mahal is more beautiful than the Empire State Building.
8. Reykjavik is more expensive than Paris.

EXERCISE 3

1. Iceland has the smallest population for its size in Europe.
2. Alaska is the largest state in the United States.
3. Vatican City is the smallest country in the world.
4. Mount Everest is the highest mountain in the world.
5. The Nile is the longest river in the world.
6. Death Valley in California is the hottest place in the United States.
7. Tokyo is one of the most expensive cities in the world.
8. Acapulco is the most popular city in Mexico for tourists.

EXERCISE 4

Answers will vary.

EXERCISE 5

Inga Stefansson is from Iceland. Iceland is a country in Europe. She speaks Icelandic. This language is similar to German. Life in Iceland is the **most expensive** in Europe. But people are healthy, and they live the **longest** lives.

Additional Writing Skills Activity

Have students work in pairs. Have them look back at Reading 2 and find all the superlative adjectives. For each adjective that is modified by the word "most," have students count the number of syllables in the adjective. They should find: *largest*; *hardest*; *longest*; *most expensive* (3); and *longest*.

WRITING PRACTICE pages 43–44

Answers vary throughout this section.

JOURNAL

Ask students to choose an unusual place that they would like to visit. Why do they want to go there? Ask students to try to use adjectives in their writing. This journal task will help them do the Timed Writing activity at the end of the unit.

WEAVING IT TOGETHER

TIMED WRITING page 45

Answers will vary.

SEARCH THE INTERNET page 45

A Suggested keywords:
- fascinating cities
- unusual cities
- must-see cities
- dangerous cities

B *Answers will vary.*

WHAT DO YOU THINK NOW? page 45

1. more
2. more
3. read
4. work

UNIT 3 Ways to Health

This unit deals with two unusual aspects of health: the importance of sleep and the healthful effects of laughter. One way to begin the unit might be to write the verbs "sleep" and "laugh" on the board and ask students to think of other involuntary things that humans do in certain situations. You may be able to elicit *cry*, *cough*, *sneeze*, *smile*, *breathe*, and *yawn*. Once you have a list on the board, ask students if any of these actions are good for your health.

READING ■ 1
Go to Sleep!

PRE-READING page 48

Begin the lesson in one of the following ways:

- Teach students the term "insomnia" and ask which students have trouble sleeping. Then start a discussion on what might be the causes of insomnia. Some common causes are stress, anxiety, environmental noise, sleeping during the day (napping), and drinking stimulating drinks or eating too much before going to bed.

- Ask students to think about what happens when one does not get enough sleep. You may elicit *poor concentration*, *slower reaction time*, *headaches*, and *generally feeling moody or unwell*.

- Have students look at the photo and ask them if they know about how much animals sleep compared to humans. They should know that humans sleep an average of eight hours a night. But what about other animals: horses—3; cows—4; dogs—10; cats and mice—12; lions—14. The mammal that sleeps the most is the little brown bat—20 hours a day on average.

PREPARING FOR THE READING TOPIC
Answers will vary.

KEY VOCABULARY

1. e	**3.** d	**5.** b	**7.** h
2. g	**4.** f	**6.** a	**8.** c

VOCABULARY pages 51–52
VOCABULARY IN CONTEXT

A
1. average	**5.** inventor
2. Let's say	**6.** teenager
3. fall asleep	**7.** normal
4. adult	**8.** awake

B
1. b	**3.** b	**5.** b
2. a	**4.** c	**6.** c

Answers for sentences will vary.

VOCABULARY BUILDING

A
1. dream
2. have a nightmare
3. snore

B *Answers will vary.*

READING COMPREHENSION page 52

LOOKING FOR MAIN IDEAS

Possible answers:

1. Adults need 7 to 8 hours of sleep a day.
2. *Insomnia* is the name of the problem for people who cannot sleep.
3. Benjamin Franklin and Mark Twain are two famous Americans who had a problem with sleep.

LOOKING FOR DETAILS

1. T   3. F   5. T
2. T   4. F   6. F

DISCUSSION page 53

Answers will vary.

Additional Discussion Activity

Once students have filled in the chart in the Discussion section, make sure students know how to work out the average from a set of numbers. Put students in groups and have them work out the average number of hours of sleep per night in their group. Then by finding out the average number of hours of sleep in all the groups, it will be possible to work out the average number of hours of sleep per night for the class.

CRITICAL THINKING page 53

Answers will vary.

Additional Critical Thinking Activity

Put students in pairs. Have students act out a role play. One student plays someone who has trouble sleeping. The other student plays the role of a doctor whose job it is to find out about the patient's sleep habits, to work out why the patient may not be sleeping well, and to suggest solutions.

WRITING ■ 1

WRITING SKILLS pages 54–55

EXERCISE 1

1. When I sleep, I have the radio on.
2. When I sleep, I snore.
3. When she started snoring, her husband woke up.
4. When I sleep, I like to hold something.
5. When I woke up, I was tired.
6. When I have problems, I cannot sleep.
7. When I eat too much, I have a nightmare.
8. When I went to bed, it was midnight.

EXERCISE 2

Sleep **is** very important ~~is~~. It is **more** important than food. When a person **does** not eat, he or she dies. When a person does not sleep, he or she dies **faster / more quickly**. Bab**ies** need the **most** sleep. Teenager**s** sleep **longer** than adult**s**. People need less sleep as they get **older**.

Additional Writing Skills Activity

Write five sentences on the board with clauses incorrectly reversed. For example: "When I ate dinner, I got home." Ask students to come up to the board to write correct versions. Have the rest of the class decide if each student at the board has correctly written and punctuated the sentences.

WRITING PRACTICE pages 55–56

Answers vary throughout this section.

JOURNAL

Ask students to write about their sleep habits and any tricks or remedies they use to help them get to sleep or sleep well.

READING ■ 2
Laughing Out Loud

PRE-READING   page 57

Begin the lesson in one of the following ways:

- Tell the class a couple of jokes in English. Pre-teach any vocabulary and give any background necessary first. When students don't laugh (and they probably won't!), tell them that it is very difficult to appreciate or tell a joke in a foreign language because humor is very much culturally determined. Then ask students to get into pairs to try out jokes from their own cultures on each other. Make sure that students do not tell each other offensive jokes. Have selected students tell their joke to the class. Again, remind them that they may not hear laughter!

- Ask students to work in pairs and tell each other about a recent incident in their lives or a TV show or movie that made them laugh out loud. Have students share some of their stories with the whole class.

PREPARING FOR THE READING TOPIC
Answers will vary.

KEY VOCABULARY

1. f	**3.** a	**5.** c	**7.** e
2. g	**4.** d	**6.** h	**8.** b

VOCABULARY   pages 59–60
VOCABULARY IN CONTEXT

A
1. muscles
2. organ
3. heartbeat
4. circulation
5. painkiller
6. blood pressure
7. brain
8. relaxation

B   **1.** a   **2.** c   **3.** b   **4.** b   **5.** c
Answers for sentences will vary.

VOCABULARY BUILDING

A
1. a joke
2. burst into laughter
3. embarrassed

B *Answers will vary.*

READING COMPREHENSION   pages 60–61
LOOKING FOR MAIN IDEAS

   1. a   **2.** a   **3.** c

LOOKING FOR DETAILS

1. We use <u>15</u> different muscles in our face when we laugh.
2. Laughing is good for every organ in our <u>body</u>.
3. Every minute we laugh is the same as 45 <u>minutes</u> of relaxation.
4. We may change the way we laugh in different <u>situations</u>.
5. When we laugh, we breathe <u>quickly</u>.
6. Our <u>brain</u> makes a natural painkiller.

DISCUSSION   page 61
Answers will vary.

CRITICAL THINKING   page 61
Answers will vary.

WRITING ■ 2
WRITING SKILLS   pages 62–63
EXERCISE 1

1. She laughs <u>freely</u>.
2. He laughs <u>loudly</u>.
3. She laughs <u>shyly</u>.

4. He laughs <u>nervously</u>.

5. They are studying <u>seriously</u>.

6. He speaks <u>quietly</u>.

EXERCISE 2

Answers will vary.

EXERCISE 3

Scientist**s** **are** studying laughter serious**ly**. They are finding that laughter is **good** for us. When people are sick, laughter helps them to get ~~more~~ better. Laughter club**s** started in **I**ndia. People join a laughter club and go **every** day. They may laugh loud**ly** for minutes and feel **better** afterwards.

Additional Writing Skills Activity

Write some common adverbs on pieces of paper and fold the pieces of paper up and put them in a bag. Some adverbs you can use are: *slowly, quickly, fast, carefully, softly, loudly, quietly, badly, beautifully, crazily,* and *nervously.* To make the activity easier, you can also write the adverbs on the board. Then call different students to the front of the class and tell them to pull an adverb out of the bag or secretly tell them the name of an adverb from the board. Then, also secretly, give the students an action to perform in that manner. For example, tell them to dance, write, speak, walk, sing, etc. The rest of the class guesses which action and adverb the student is performing. Tell them to make a complete sentence, such as "She is singing softly."

WRITING PRACTICE   pages 63–64

Answers vary throughout this section.

JOURNAL

Ask students to write about a funny TV show or movie or a scene in a funny TV show or movie. Ask them to describe the scene and say why they found it funny.

WEAVING IT TOGETHER

TIMED WRITING   page 65

Answers will vary.

SEARCH THE INTERNET   page 65

A Suggested keywords:
- sleep disorders
- effects of too little sleep
- sleep aids

B Suggested key words:
- funny jokes from around the world
- jokes for ESL students

WHAT DO YOU THINK NOW?   page 65

1. is

2. 16

3. lower

4. 45

UNIT 4 Customs

This unit introduces two very different types of customs. Use the unit opener photo to introduce the different meanings of the word *customs*, from everyday habits to celebrations and ceremonies.

READING ■ 1
What to Name the Baby

PRE-READING page 68

Begin the lesson in one of the following ways:

- Talk about your own name and its meaning.

- Have students tell their partner the meaning of their name and how their name was chosen for them. Walk around the room as students are doing this and listen for vocabulary or grammar structures that students need help with.

- Ask for volunteers to give a brief report on what they found out about their partner's name.

- Use students' suggestions to compile a list of popular first names. What are the most common origins of names? Try to categorize them.

PREPARING FOR THE READING TOPIC
Answers will vary.

KEY VOCABULARY

1. g	**3.** e	**5.** d	**7.** c
2. a	**4.** f	**6.** h	**8.** b

VOCABULARY pages 70–71
VOCABULARY IN CONTEXT

A
1. ceremonies	**5.** planets
2. tongue	**6.** horoscope
3. honey	**7.** suggests
4. priests	**8.** blesses

B *Answers will vary.*

VOCABULARY BUILDING

1. suggest	**4.** blessing
2. suggestion	**5.** pray
3. bless	**6.** prayers

READING COMPREHENSION pages 71–72
LOOKING FOR MAIN IDEAS
Possible answers:

1. The Hindu religion has 16 special ceremonies for important times in a person's life.

2. Hindu people have a baby naming ceremony after a baby is born.

3. The priest visits the family to name the baby, to read the baby's fortune, and to bless the baby.

LOOKING FOR DETAILS

1. F	**3.** T	**5.** T
2. T	**4.** F	**6.** F

DISCUSSION page 72

Answers will vary.

CRITICAL THINKING page 72

Answers will vary.

WRITING ■ 1

WRITING SKILLS pages 73–75

EXERCISE 1

1. C	**7.** C
2. NC	**8.** C
3. C	**9.** C
4. NC	**10.** NC
5. C	**11.** NC
6. C	**12.** C and NC

EXERCISE 2

1. a	**5.** some
2. some	**6.** some
3. a	**7.** some
4. an	**8.** an

EXERCISE 3

Answers will vary.

EXERCISE 4

There are about one **billion** people in India. Most of the people are of the **Hindu** religion. This is the **largest** religion in Asia. It is also the world's **oldest** religion. **A** person cannot become a Hindu. You are born Hindu or you are not. There are also **M**uslims, **C**hristians, and other religion**s** in India.

WRITING PRACTICE pages 75–76

Answers vary throughout this section.

JOURNAL

Ask students to write about the meaning of their name and how their name was chosen. Do they like their name? Why or why not? If they could choose another name, which name would they choose and why?

READING ▪ 2
Eat, Drink, and Know the Customs

PRE-READING   page 77

Begin the lesson in one of the following ways:

- Talk about different greeting customs in different cultures.

- Discuss customs relating to being a guest at another person's home.

- Have students look at the photo and describe how the people are eating.

- Ask students to guess what kind of table customs they think are common in Thailand. How might these customs be different from those in their country? Discuss some differences in table customs in various countries.

PREPARING FOR THE READING TOPIC

Answers will vary.

KEY VOCABULARY

1. b	**3.** e	**5.** h	**7.** f
2. d	**4.** a	**6.** c	**8.** g

VOCABULARY   pages 79–80

VOCABULARY IN CONTEXT

A
1. chopsticks	5. insists
2. bowl	6. refill
3. host	7. keep an eye on
4. offer	8. at the middle

B *Answers will vary.*

VOCABULARY BUILDING

A 1. off
2. down
3. up

B *Answers will vary.*

READING COMPREHENSION   pages 80–81

LOOKING FOR MAIN IDEAS

1. c   2. b   3. a

LOOKING FOR DETAILS

1. The Thai <u>do not</u> use knives when they eat. **OR** The Thai use <u>forks and spoons</u> when they eat.

2. If you are right-handed, you must keep your fork in your <u>left</u> hand. **OR** If you are right-handed, you must keep your <u>spoon</u> in your right hand.

3. The first time your host offers you more food, you must say <u>no</u>.

4. You should refill your <u>neighbor's</u> glass.

5. If you need to cut food, you use your <u>spoon</u>.

6. If you do not want more food, you must <u>leave</u> some food on your plate.

DISCUSSION   page 81

Answers will vary.

Additional Discussion Activity

Have students work in groups to make a list of the five most important rules for eating politely in their culture. Compare the lists and discuss any disagreements or contradictions.

CRITICAL THINKING   page 81

Answers will vary.

WRITING ■ 2

WRITING SKILLS   pages 82–83

EXERCISE 1

1. at
2. with
3. in
4. at
5. in
6. with

EXERCISE 2

1. Use the side <u>of your spoon</u>.
2. Table customs are different all <u>over the world</u>.
3. Keep the fork <u>in your left hand</u>.
4. People usually serve rice <u>in a separate bowl</u>.
5. The most important place <u>at a table</u> is <u>at the middle</u>.
6. It is good to leave a little food <u>on your plate</u>.

EXERCISE 3

Thai food is **delicious**. Thai people eat a lot of vegetable**s**, seafood, **rice**, and noodles. Thai food is often spicy. The **T**hai usually have breakfast from seven thirty to nine **in** the morning. When they eat breakfast**,** they have **tea** and rice. They drink tea without **sugar**, **milk**, or lemon. The Thai do not eat **cheese**.

Additional Writing Skills Activity 1

Ask a volunteer to step outside the classroom. Hide a coin or some other prize somewhere in the classroom, preferably under something else. When the student returns, he or she must try to find the object by asking questions of other members of the class. Tell the student that he or she should use a preposition in each question—for example, "Is the coin near the teacher's desk?" "Is it under a book?" To make the game more challenging, allow no more than five questions.

Additional Writing Skills Activity 2

Pass out large sheets of paper and markers of assorted colors. Ask students to draw a diagram of a room in their home. The diagram should show the position of furniture and other objects. You may want to draw one of your own living room as an example. Tell students to leave enough space at the bottom of the page to write five sentences about the room. Each sentence should use a preposition—for example, "The television is in front of the couch."

WRITING PRACTICE   pages 83–84

Answers vary throughout this section.

WEAVING IT TOGETHER

TIMED WRITING   page 85

Answers will vary.

SEARCH THE INTERNET   page 85

A Suggested keywords:
- name meanings
- name origins
- name roots

B *Answers will vary.*

WHAT DO YOU THINK NOW?   page 85

1. 16
2. names
3. a spoon and fork
4. is not

UNIT 5 Food

In this unit, students read about an uncommon and unusual food and a common and highly popular drink. The unit opener photo shows popcorn popping in slow motion. Talk about the photo. Ask students if they like popcorn. Ask them what other snack foods they like to eat. Ask students to make lists of foods that they like and are good for them, foods that they like that are not good for them, and foods that they don't like that are good for them. Have students share their lists in pairs, groups, or with the whole class.

READING ▪ 1
Hold Your Nose and Eat!

PRE-READING page 88

Begin the lesson in one of the following ways:

- Have students write the alphabet down on a piece of paper, putting one letter on each line. Give students a time limit, say five minutes, and ask them to write down the name of one fruit in English for each letter of the alphabet. See who can fill in the most letters.

- Have students look at the photo on pages 88–89 and the title of the reading and have them predict what the reading might be about.

PREPARING FOR THE READING TOPIC
Answers will vary.

KEY VOCABULARY

1. g	**3.** d	**5.** f	**7.** e
2. h	**4.** c	**6.** b	**8.** a

VOCABULARY pages 90–91

VOCABULARY IN CONTEXT

A
1. hate	5. weigh
2. produces	6. carefully
3. terrible	7. popular
4. allow	8. competitions

B *Answers will vary.*

VOCABULARY BUILDING

1. weigh	4. produces
2. weight	5. careful
3. product	6. carefully

READING COMPREHENSION page 92

LOOKING FOR MAIN IDEAS
Possible answers:

1. The durian is famous for its terrible smell.

2. Many Asian countries do not allow the durian in taxis, buses, trains, planes, elevators, stores, or hotels.

3. There is a nine-day festival for the durian in Thailand.

LOOKING FOR DETAILS

1. F   3. F   5. T
2. F   4. T   6. F

DISCUSSION   page 92

Answers will vary.

CRITICAL THINKING   page 92

Answers will vary.

WRITING ■ 1

WRITING SKILLS   pages 93–94

EXERCISE 1

1. 4
2. 3
3. 1
4. 5
5. 2

EXERCISE 2

Possible answers:

1. First, wash the grapefruit.
2. Then cut the grapefruit in half.
3. Next, put some sugar or salt on top of the grapefruit.
4. Then cut out pieces of the grapefruit with a spoon or small knife.
5. Finally, eat the grapefruit.

EXERCISE 3

Answers will vary.

EXERCISE 4

My **f**amily love**s** to eat durian. My mother always find**s** good durian. Last week, she made a **c**ake with **a** frozen durian**s**. That day two **A**merican visitor**s** came to our **h**ouse. She gave them some durian **c**ake. They liked it very much.

WRITING PRACTICE   pages 94–95

Answers vary throughout this section.

JOURNAL

Ask students to write about their healthy and unhealthy eating habits. Have them explain why a particular habit is healthy or unhealthy.

READING ■ 2
The World's Most Popular Drink

PRE-READING   page 96

Begin the lesson in one of the following ways:

- Have students conduct a class survey of coffee drinking habits. Have students come up with ideas for questions and help them make them grammatical. Students then interview each other to find out what percentage of the class drinks coffee, how many cups a day people drink, whether they have milk or sugar in their coffee, etc.

- Have a discussion with the class about coffee houses or shops in their country or the country that they are currently in. How popular are they? What else happens in them besides drinking coffee? What age group goes to them? How much does a cup of coffee cost? What different types of coffee drink are served?

PREPARING FOR THE READING TOPIC

Answers will vary.

KEY VOCABULARY

1. b	**3.** g	**5.** h	**7.** c
2. f	**4.** e	**6.** a	**8.** d

VOCABULARY pages 99–100

VOCABULARY IN CONTEXT

A
1. discovered	**5.** too
2. took care of	**6.** beans
3. plants	**7.** boil
4. excited	**8.** liquid

B
1. c	**3.** a	**5.** c
2. b	**4.** b	

Answers for sentences will vary.

VOCABULARY BUILDING

1. discover	**4.** excitement
2. discovery	**5.** liquefy
3. excited	**6.** liquid

READING COMPREHENSION pages 100–101

LOOKING FOR MAIN IDEAS

1. b **2.** a **3.** c

LOOKING FOR DETAILS

1. The German name for coffee is *Kaffee*.

2. The people of Sweden drink more than five cups of coffee a day.

3. When the goats ate the coffee plants, they could not / couldn't sleep well that night.

4. The word *coffee* comes from an Arabic word.

5. Voltaire drank 72 cups of coffee every day.

6. Many coffee shops also give customers free Wi-Fi.

Additional Reading Activity

Write the following numbers on the board: 5, 700, 1200, 72, 1735, and 60. Give students three minutes to scan the reading to find the numbers and what they refer to. Now have students close their books and see which students can tell you what the numbers from the reading refer to.

DISCUSSION page 101

Answers will vary.

CRITICAL THINKING page 101

Answers will vary.

WRITING ▪ 2

WRITING SKILLS pages 102–103

EXERCISE 1

1. People all over the world drink coffee. It is the world's most popular drink. The French call it *café*, the Germans *Kaffee*, the Japanese *koohi*, the Turkish *kahve*. But the people of Sweden drink the most coffee—more than five cups a day. Over half of American adults drink it every day, but not as much as in Sweden. Too much coffee is bad for your health.

2. Three

3. Coffee

EXERCISE 2

1. Jack loves coffee. He drinks it every morning.

2. I can't drink coffee at night. It keeps me awake.

3. I usually have coffee with milk, but sometimes I have it with cream.

4. At 4:00 every afternoon, my friend eats cookies. She likes to eat <u>them</u> with a cup of coffee.

EXERCISE 3

Tony always drink**s** **hot** coffee. He drinks **it** with milk**,** but no **sugar**. He doesn't like **strong coffee** like **T**urkish coffee. His **f**avorite is **B**razilian coffee. He drinks four small cups every day. He has a cup for breakfast and a cup at eleven o'clock. After lunch, he has another cup. When he gets home from work**,** he has a final cup**s**.

Additional Writing Skills Activity

Ask students to take out a sheet of paper and write six kinds of food and drink on it. You may want to give examples. Encourage the use of both count and noncount nouns. Give examples such as *chocolate*, *tea*, *fish*, *grapes*, *apples*, *bananas*, *hamburgers*, and *butter*. Tell students to write two or three sentences about each food. Tell them in the second and third sentence they should use a pronoun. Give them an example: *I like tea. I drink it with milk. I usually drink it in the morning after I get up.* Go around the room and check to see if students are using pronouns correctly.

WRITING PRACTICE   pages 103–104

Answers vary throughout this section.

JOURNAL

Ask students to write about meals that they had in the last week. Ask them to include what they drank with the meals. Prompt them to write about what they liked or did not like about the meals, whether or not the meals contained traditional foods from their culture, whether or not they prepared any of the food themselves, and whether any of the food was a fast food or not.

WEAVING IT TOGETHER

TIMED WRITING   page 105

Answers will vary.

SEARCH THE INTERNET   page 105

A *Answers will vary.*

B Suggested keywords:
- drinking coffee around the world
- preparing coffee around the world
- world's best coffee shops

WHAT DO YOU THINK NOW?   page 105

1. is	**3.** first started
2. years	**4.** Swedish people

UNIT 6 — Inventors and Their Inventions

The readings in this unit focus on some inventions that have changed the daily lives of millions of people and the stories of the inventors who created them. Begin the unit by asking students which inventions they think have changed people's daily lives in the past 100 years, 50 years, or even 10 years.

READING ■ 1
Dinner Fresh from the Freezer

PRE-READING page 108

Begin the lesson in one of the following ways:

- Have students look at the photos on pages 108 and 109 and read the title of the reading. Ask students to predict what the reading may be about and what the life of the man in the photo might have been like.

- Ask students what they would invent that could revolutionize the food industry today. Encourage them to use their imaginations and be as creative as possible.

PREPARING FOR THE READING TOPIC
Answers will vary.

KEY VOCABULARY

1. f	**3.** a	**5.** g	**7.** b
2. h	**4.** d	**6.** e	**8.** c

Additional Pre-Reading Activity

Have students write down the following dates in a horizontal list on a piece of paper: 1886, 1912, 1917, 1924, and 1930. Now tell students that they are going to skim the reading to find out what happened in those years. Explain how they are not to read the passage carefully. They are only to find those dates and find what happened in those years. Tell students that they will only have a few minutes to do this. Have them write notes next to the dates and then close their books and report their answers back to you.

VOCABULARY pages 111–112
VOCABULARY IN CONTEXT

A
1. frozen food	**5.** delicious
2. fur	**6.** diet
3. convenient	**7.** try out
4. taste	**8.** curiosity

B *Answers will vary.*

VOCABULARY BUILDING

1. convenience	**4.** tasty
2. convenient	**5.** curiosity
3. taste	**6.** curious

READING COMPREHENSION page 112–113

LOOKING FOR MAIN IDEAS

1. a   **2.** b   **3.** c

LOOKING FOR DETAILS

1. Birdseye was one of <u>eight</u> children.

2. In <u>1912</u>, Birdseye went to Canada.

3. Birdseye bought and sold <u>fur</u> in Canada.

4. After Birdseye returned to the United States, he worked for a <u>fish</u> company.

5. Birdseye started a company called Birdseye <u>Seafoods</u>.

6. Shoppers saw frozen foods for the first time in <u>1930</u>.

DISCUSSION page 113

Answers will vary.

CRITICAL THINKING page 113

Answers will vary.

WRITING ■ 1

WRITING SKILLS pages 114–116

EXERCISE 1

1. Frozen peas are as tasty as fresh peas.

2. Fast food is not as healthy as fresh food.

3. Fresh food is not as popular as fast food.

4. Fast food is not as expensive as fresh food.

5. Frozen dessert is as good as fresh dessert.

6. Frozen fish is as well-liked as fresh fish.

EXERCISE 2

Possible answers:

1. A microwave oven is not as big as a refrigerator.

2. A microwave oven is not as expensive as a refrigerator.

3. A microwave oven is as important as a freezer.

EXERCISE 3

We often **call** a refrigerator a "fridge." **It** is a very **convenient** appliance in our homes. The **r**efrigerator for the home start**ed** around 1850. Before the refrigerator, people used **ice** to keep food cool. They bought **ice** and put the **ice** in **i**ceboxes. They like**d** their iceboxes and didn't want to buy refrigerators!

Additional Writing Skills Activity

Have students write five sentences comparing different foods using "not as . . . as" and the following adjectives: *tasty, delicious, expensive, sweet,* and *chewy.*

WRITING PRACTICE pages 116–117

Answers vary throughout this section.

JOURNAL

If in the pre-reading you asked students to come up with an invention to revolutionize the food industry or food preparation, have students write about their invention. Otherwise, ask students to write about what frozen foods they like to eat and don't like to eat.

READING ■ 2
A Sharp Idea from King Gillette

PRE-READING page 118

Begin the lesson in one of the following ways:

- Explain the term "disposable" and ask students to name some things that they use that are disposable. Then discuss what kind of impact students think so many disposable products have on the environment.

- Explain the term "disposable" and find out if students are aware of trends that involve using more recyclable and reusable things, such as canvas shopping bags. Ask them to name some products that are recyclable and reusable.

- Have students look at the photo on page 119 and read the photo caption and the title of the reading. Ask students to predict what the reading may be about.

PREPARING FOR THE READING TOPIC
Answers will vary.

KEY VOCABULARY

1. e	**3.** d	**5.** b	**7.** f
2. h	**4.** g	**6.** a	**8.** c

VOCABULARY pages 120–121
VOCABULARY IN CONTEXT

A
1. household name	**5.** encouraged
2. dull	**6.** disposable
3. blade	**7.** product
4. invention	**8.** sharpen

B *Answers will vary.*

VOCABULARY BUILDING

1. invent	**4.** encouragement
2. invention	**5.** product
3. encourage	**6.** produce

READING COMPREHENSION page 122
LOOKING FOR MAIN IDEAS
Possible answers:

1. When Gillette was a salesman, he wanted to be an inventor.

2. Gillette wanted to make a razor with a safe, removable blade.

3. Gillette sold so many razors because he had a good product and a good idea. He also knew how to advertise.

LOOKING FOR DETAILS

1. F	**3.** T	**5.** F
2. T	**4.** T	**6.** T

Additional Reading Activity

Tell students that sometimes the writer tells the reader what age Gillette was when something happened, and sometimes the writer tells the reader the year something happened. Ask students to do some math and find out both the year the following events happened as well as Gillette's age at the time. Have students create the following chart in their notebooks. Have them look back at the caption to the photo on page 119. It contains important information that can help them.

Year	Gillette's Age	What happened
		Gillette left school.
		The president of the company Gillette was working for wanted him to invent something disposable.
		Gillette started a company with William Emery Nickerson.
		Gillette renamed the company.
		The company sold 51 razors.
		The company sold almost a 100,000 razors.
		Gillette became a millionaire.
		The U.S. stock market crashed.
		Gillette died.

DISCUSSION page 122

Answers will vary.

CRITICAL THINKING page 122

Answers will vary.

WRITING ■ 2

WRITING SKILLS pages 123–124

EXERCISE 1

1. very
2. too
3. too
4. very
5. too
6. very

EXERCISE 2

1. It is too strong.
2. It has a strong smell, too.
3. It makes your teeth whiter, too.
4. It is too expensive.
5. It makes my hair shiny, too.
6. It has too many chemicals.

EXERCISE 3

The Chinese invent**ed** toothbrushes. Th**ese [The]** toothbrushes had animal hair because there was no **nylon** at that time. In 1938, people started to use nylon toothbrushes. Today we can buy **many** types and colors of toothbrushes. But in some **A**frican and **S**outh **A**merican countr**ies**, people still use **t**ree branches to care for their **teeth**.

Additional Writing Skills Activity

Write sentences on pieces of paper and cut them into strips and fold them. Each piece of paper contains a sentence that students can mime out, for example: *This suitcase is too heavy to carry.* or *This tea is too hot to drink.* Give the sentences to students to act out and have the class guess what sentence is being acted out. As a follow-up, have students write their own sentences and act them out for the class to guess.

WRITING PRACTICE pages 125–126

Answers vary throughout this section.

JOURNAL

Ask students to write about some disposable products that they would have a hard time living without, and why.

WEAVING IT TOGETHER

TIMED WRITING page 127

Answers will vary.

SEARCH THE INTERNET page 127

A *Answers will vary.*

B Suggested keywords:
- Jacob Schick
- Schick razors
- the Schick razor company

WHAT DO YOU THINK NOW? page 127

1. liked
2. is
3. razor blade
4. picture

UNIT 7 Amazing People

This unit focuses on the achievements of two unusual women. They are both scientists, although in very different fields. Begin the unit by having students think about the title of the unit: What makes an "amazing person"? Then look at the unit opener photo. Ask students what they know about the Nobel Prize. Do they know in what fields the prizes are given? Do they know the names of any Nobel Prize winners?

READING ■ 1
Hayat Sindi: One Person Helps the World

PRE-READING   page 130

Begin the lesson in one of the following ways:

• Pre-teach the word "admire," and then ask students to make a list of people in the world or their country whom they admire. They should not be family or friends, but public figures. Then have them look at their list and choose the three people on the list that they most admire. Tell them that they are going to have to say why they admire these people. Then put students in pairs to tell each other who they admire and why. Ask each student to talk to the whole class about one of the people they admire.

• Look at the title of the reading. Have students think about how one person can help the world.

PREPARING FOR THE READING TOPIC
Answers will vary.

KEY VOCABULARY

1. f	**3.** h	**5.** g	**7.** a
2. e	**4.** c	**6.** d	**8.** b

VOCABULARY   pages 132–133
VOCABULARY IN CONTEXT

A
1. disease	**5.** scientist
2. blood	**6.** attended
3. postage stamp	**7.** winner
4. list	**8.** graduated

B *Answers will vary.*

VOCABULARY BUILDING

1. attend	**4.** graduate
2. attendance	**5.** winner
3. graduation	**6.** win

READING COMPREHENSION   page 134
LOOKING FOR MAIN IDEAS

1. b   **2.** a   **3.** b

LOOKING FOR DETAILS

1. Sindi told her parents she wanted to go to <u>England</u> to study.

2. Sindi graduated from King's College in <u>1995</u>.

3. Sindi's invention is a piece of <u>paper</u> the size of a postage stamp.

4. Sindi's invention works on diseases of the <u>kidney</u> and liver.

5. In 2010, Sindi won the Prince Khalid Award for her work in <u>science</u>.
6. In 2009, Sindi worked at <u>Harvard</u> University.

DISCUSSION   page 135

Answers will vary.

CRITICAL THINKING   page 135

Answers will vary.

WRITING ▪ 1

WRITING SKILLS   pages 136–137

EXERCISE 1

Possible answers:

1. Where were you born?
2. When were you born?
3. What does your father do?

4. Who is an important person in your life?
5. How many brothers and sisters do you have?
6. Where did you go to high school?
7. When did you graduate from high school?
8. What are you doing right now?
9. What do you want to do in the future?
10. Why do you want to go to an American university?

EXERCISE 2

1. in	**5.** for
2. for	**6.** from, to
3. from, to	**7.** in
4. in	**8.** for

EXERCISE 3

In 1991, Hayat Sindi went to **E**ngland. She stud**ied E**nglish and enter**ed** King's College in **L**ondon. She graduat**ed** in 1995. After that, she went **to** Cambridge University. Sindi made **science** education important for girls in the **M**iddle **E**ast.

WRITING PRACTICE   pages 138–139

Answers vary throughout this section.

Ask students to write about a public figure who they admire. Tell them to write some details about the person's life and to write about why they admire the person.

READING ▪ 2
A Life with Chimpanzees

PRE-READING page 140

Begin the lesson in one of the following ways:

- Explain to the class the difference between a "wild animal" and a "domesticated animal." Ask students to tell you the names of each type of animal. Explain the term "tame" to the class. Ask students which animals are sometimes "tame" and which animals are not easy to tame.

- Have students look at the title of the reading, the photo, and the caption. Have students predict who the woman in the photo is and why she is sitting so near chimpanzees. Have students predict some details of the woman's life.

PREPARING FOR THE READING TOPIC

Answers will vary.

KEY VOCABULARY

1. e	**3.** b	**5.** g	**7.** f
2. d	**4.** a	**6.** c	**8.** h

VOCABULARY pages 142–143

VOCABULARY IN CONTEXT

A
1. desire
2. patient
3. tools
4. save
5. experience
6. articles
7. made plans
8. environment

B *Answers will vary.*

VOCABULARY BUILDING

1. experience
2. experienced
3. environment
4. environmental
5. patient
6. patience

READING COMPREHENSION pages 144–145

LOOKING FOR MAIN IDEAS

Possible answers:

1. She loved to read stories about Africa and wanted to go there one day.

2. She didn't know anything about chimpanzees.

3. She returned to Tanzania and continued her work.

LOOKING FOR DETAILS

1. F	**3.** T	**5.** T
2. F	**4.** T	**6.** F

Additional Reading Skills Activity

Put students in small groups. Write the 10 sentences in the last paragraph of the reading on 10 strips of paper. Make as many copies of the 10 sentences as there are groups in the class. Tell students to close their books. Now have students put the 10 sentences in the correct order.

DISCUSSION page 145

Answers will vary.

CRITICAL THINKING page 145

Answers will vary.

JOURNAL

Ask students to write about unusual or rare wild animals in their country. Have them describe any special characteristics of these animals and if they are endangered and why.

WRITING ■ 2

WRITING SKILLS pages 146–147

EXERCISE 1

Answers will vary.

EXERCISE 2

Possible answers:

1. When she was 23
2. Three years later
3. At age 28
4. Four years later
5. When she was 43
6. At age 68

EXERCISE 3

Wild **c**himpanzees **live** only in **A**frica. We find them in 21 count**ries** in Africa. These count**ries** are mostly in the **c**enter of Africa where there **are** rainforests. In these rainforest**s**, **c**himpanzees can live to be 50 year**s** old.

WRITING PRACTICE page 148

Answers vary throughout this section.

WEAVING IT TOGETHER

TIMED WRITING page 149

Answers will vary.

SEARCH THE INTERNET page 149

A *Answers will vary.*

B Suggested keywords:
- Dian Fossey
- Jane Goodall

WHAT DO YOU THINK NOW? page 149

1. can
2. can
3. tools
4. sometimes kill

UNIT 8 Readings from Literature

In this unit, students read and study a poem and a fable. You could introduce the unit by asking students to make a list of different types of readings and literary forms: fiction and nonfiction, novels, poems, short stories, biographies, magazine articles, etc. Find out what your students like to read. Students may recommend something that they have read recently that they enjoyed reading.

READING ■ 1
The Rain

PRE-READING page 152

Begin the lesson in one of the following ways:

• With books closed, read the poem to students or play the audio, but do not let students hear the title of the poem. Ask them to come up with a title for the poem.

• Have students look at the picture on page 153 and brainstorm words that are related in some way to rain. Put their words up on the board.

PREPARING FOR THE READING TOPIC

Answers will vary.

KEY VOCABULARY

1. c	**3.** d	**5.** h	**7.** e
2. g	**4.** f	**6.** b	**8.** a

VOCABULARY pages 154–155
VOCABULARY IN CONTEXT

A 1. dark
2. sight
3. fill
4. leaves
5. drop
6. on top
7. beneath
8. bright

B 1. a. A tree often has leaves.
2. b. We often fill a cup.
3. b. The color black is dark.
4. c. Potatoes grow beneath the ground.
5. c. A field of snow is a bright place.

VOCABULARY BUILDING

1. c	**3.** a	**5.** d
2. f	**4.** b	**6.** e

READING COMPREHENSION page 155
UNDERSTANDING THE POEM

Possible answers:

1. In the poem, the rain is falling on the leaves.

2. The writer thinks the leaves are drinking the rain.

3. The writer likes the sound of drops on the leaves.

4. After the rain stops, the sun will come out and make everything bright.

FINDING THE MEANING OF THE POEM

Answers will vary.

DISCUSSION page 156

Answers will vary.

CRITICAL THINKING page 156

Answers will vary.

WRITING ▪ 1

WRITING SKILLS pages 157–158

EXERCISE 1

1. c	**4.** a	**7.** a	**10.** b
2. b	**5.** c	**8.** b	**11.** a
3. c	**6.** b	**9.** c	**12.** c

EXERCISE 2

William **H**enry Davies was born in Wales. Wales is a part of the **U**nited **K**ingdom. He worked at different jobs in his **life**. He travel**ed** to the United States and **C**anada. He return**ed** to the United Kingdom and wrote poems and books. Davies was never **rich**. He die**d** in 1940.

WRITING PRACTICE pages 158–159

Answers vary throughout this section.

JOURNAL

Ask students to write about their personal response to the poem "Rain." Ask them to write about if they liked the poem. Why or why not?

READING ▪ 2
The Shepherd's Boy

PRE-READING page 160

Begin the lesson in one of the following ways:

• Have students look at the photo. Ask them to describe it. Have them imagine where the boy is, what his job is, and how old he is.

• Have students look at the title of the reading and make sure they understand what a "shepherd" is and does. It is also important that they understand the meaning of the word "wolf" before they start reading. After finding out what *shepherd* and *wolf* mean, perhaps students will be able to predict what the story will be about.

• On the board, write the word "sheep." Have students help you make a word cluster with the word "sheep" in the middle. Elicit: *wool*, *shepherd*, *flock*, *fields*, and any other words that students may know that they might associate with sheep.

PREPARING FOR THE READING TOPIC
Answers will vary.

KEY VOCABULARY

1. b	**3.** a	**5.** h	**7.** d
2. c	**4.** g	**6.** e	**8.** f

VOCABULARY pages 162–163

VOCABULARY IN CONTEXT

A
1. deceiving
2. excitement
3. truth
4. company
5. pleased
6. lie
7. trick
8. complained

B *Answers will vary.*

VOCABULARY BUILDING

1. excited
2. excitement
3. true
4. truth
5. complain
6. complaint

READING COMPREHENSION page 164

UNDERSTANDING THE FABLE

Possible answers:

1. The boy tended his sheep at the foot of a mountain near a dark forest.

2. The boy thought of a plan so he could get a little company and some excitement.

3. The boy got the villagers to come and help him by rushing down toward the village, calling out "Wolf! Wolf!"

4. When a real wolf came out of the forest the boy cried out "Wolf! Wolf!" still louder than before.

FINDING THE MEANING OF THE FABLE

Answers will vary.

Additional Reading Activity

Prepare the following versions of another fable: "The Swan and the Goose." Have students work in pairs and hand out a copy of version A to one student and version B to the other. Students should not look at each other's paper. Have them read their stories to each other, while their partner fills in the missing words. Finally, have them check their answers by looking at each other's paper.

The Swan and the Goose (version A)

A rich man went to a market and bought a goose and a _____. He fed the goose in order to fatten it and eat it one day. _____ kept the swan because of its song. When the time came for killing the _____, the cook went to get him in the dark of the night. He was not _____ to distinguish one bird from the other. By mistake, he caught the swan _____ of the goose. The swan, threatened with death, began singing. He made himself _____ by his voice and saved his life by his melody.

The Swan and the Goose (version B)

A rich man went to a _____ and bought a goose and a swan. He fed the goose in order to _____ it and eat it one day. He kept the swan because of its _____. When the time came for killing the goose, the cook went to get him in the _____ of the night. He was not able to distinguish one bird from the _____. By mistake, he caught the swan instead of the goose. The swan, threatened _____ death, began singing. He made himself known by his voice and saved his _____ by his melody.

DISCUSSION page 164
Answers will vary.

CRITICAL THINKING page 164
Answers will vary.

WRITING ▪ 2

WRITING SKILLS   pages 165–167

EXERCISE 1
Possible answers:

1. He had an idea of how to get some people to visit him and have some fun.
2. There was once a Shepherd's Boy who took care of sheep at the bottom of a mountain near a dark forest.
3. He ran to the village, calling out "Wolf! Wolf!" and the villages helped him.
4. This made the boy so happy that a few days later he did the trick again . . .
5. But soon, a real Wolf came from the forest . . .

EXERCISE 2
Possible answers:

1. A long time ago
2. old
3. died
4. tell
5. am dead
6. money and gold
7. hot
8. didn't understand
9. happily forever

EXERCISE 3
Possible answers:

1. When I talk too much, I may tell a lie.
2. If you help me, I'll help you.
3. Think carefully before you do something risky or dangerous.
4. We show what we really mean by the way we act rather than by the words we say.
5. If a man is poor but has children, he is rich in ways other than having money. His children bring him joy and give meaning to his life.

EXERCISE 4

We do not know **too** much about Aesop because he lived a long time ago. He lived in **Africa**. He was not a **free** man; he was a **slave**. Later, he became a **free** man and went to **Greece**. There, he worked for the king as an ambassador. When he worked for the king**,** some people **got** angry at him and killed him. But Aesop did not do anything wrong. Later, they made a **statue** of Aesop in Greece to remember **him**.

WRITING PRACTICE   page 168
Answers vary throughout this section.

JOURNAL

Ask students to write about their personal response to the fable "The Shepherd's Boy." Ask them to write about if they liked the fable. Why, or why not?

WEAVING IT TOGETHER

TIMED WRITING   page 169
Answers will vary.

SEARCH THE INTERNET   page 169

A *Answers will vary.*

B Suggested keywords:
- Aesop's fables
- Famous fables
- Stories by Nasreddin

WHAT DO YOU THINK NOW?   page 169

1. don't always
2. can
3. fables
4. has

Notes

Notes

LEVEL 2

Teaching Hints
and Answer Key

LEVEL 2

UNIT 1

Your Personality

In this opening unit, students learn to talk and write about their own personalities and those of people they know. They read about the influence of the left and right sides of the brain on personality and how the Chinese believe that you can tell a person's personality from the shape of his or her head.

READING ■ 1
Right Brain, Left Brain

PRE-READING page 4

Begin the lesson in one of the following ways:

- Have each student tell you how many people are in their families, including themselves, and how many of them are left-handed. Add up the total number of family members mentioned by all the students and the total number of left-handers mentioned. Divide the total number of left-handers by the total number of people and multiply by a hundred to see if the percentage of left-handers in the class's families is similar to the global average, which is estimated to be about ten percent.

- Have students talk about what left-handedness means in their culture. Are left-handed people treated differently? Do parents and teachers try to make left-handed people become right-handed?

- Ask several students to come to the board and to try to write their name with the hand they don't usually use for writing. Ask them to tell how it feels. Then have them write their name with their normal hand. Are there any students who are almost ambidextrous?

PREPARING FOR THE READING TOPIC
Answers will vary.

KEY VOCABULARY

1. h	**3.** a	**5.** f	**7.** e
2. d	**4.** g	**6.** b	**8.** c

VOCABULARY pages 7–8
VOCABULARY IN CONTEXT

A
1. have something in common
2. population
3. message
4. logic
5. in order
6. recognize
7. punctual
8. exceptions

B *Answers will vary.*

VOCABULARY BUILDING

1. exception	4. population
2. exceptional	5. recognize
3. populous	6. recognition

READING COMPREHENSION pages 8–9
LOOKING FOR MAIN IDEAS

1. b   **2.** a   **3.** c

LOOKING FOR DETAILS

1.	F	**3.**	F	**5.**	T
2.	T	**4.**	T	**6.**	F

Additional Reading Activity

Divide the class into four groups. Assign each group to one of the following paragraphs: 2, 3, 4, or 5. Tell students that they are to summarize orally for the rest of the class the contents of their paragraph. Tell students not to write down their summaries, but to prepare to speak without notes. Move around the room and help groups as needed. Have students choose one representative from their group to tell the class about the contents of their paragraph.

DISCUSSION page 9

Answers will vary.

Additional Discussion Activity

Have students review the reading and make two lists. One will list the characteristics of right-handed people; the other will list the characteristics of left-handed people. Have students check the characteristics that they think apply to them and to tell the rest of the class about their results.

CRITICAL THINKING page 9

Answers will vary.

WRITING ■ 1

WRITING SKILLS pages 10–13

EXERCISE 1

1.	F	**3.**	F	**5.**	T
2.	T	**4.**	F		

EXERCISE 2

1. **St. M**ary's **C**ollege is located in **B**oston, **M**assachusetts.

2. **I**n **A**ugust 1959, **H**awaii became the fiftieth state of the **U**nited **S**tates.

3. **I** parked my car on the corner of **G**reenwood **A**venue and **L**exington.

4. **M**aria is a student from **P**eru. **S**he speaks **S**panish, **F**rench, and **I**talian.

5. **T**here are no classes during **C**hristmas, **E**aster, or **T**hanksgiving vacations.

6. **S**tudents who are **B**uddhist, **M**uslim, **C**hristian, and **J**ewish all got together to help.

7. **I** am taking three classes this semester: **E**nglish 120, **S**panish 1A, and **B**usiness **A**dministration.

8. **H**ave you been to see the **W**hite **H**ouse in **W**ashington, **D.C.**?

EXERCISE 3

Possible answers:

1. Eating in the United States of America
2. The Importance of Learning English
3. The Most Important Day of My Life
4. Living Away from Home

EXERCISE 4

There are more than 500 million left-handed people in the world. There are also many left-handers who are famous. Recent **A**merican president**s** who are left-handed are Ronald Reagan, **B**ill Clinton, and Barack **O**bama. Actors such as **T**om Cruise and **R**obert De Niro and women like **Q**ueen Elizabeth II and **N**icole Kidman **are** also left-handed. In the old days, people thought left-handed people were bad. In **J**apan a long time ago, a man could ask for a divorce if he found that his wife was left-handed. Today, it's not bad to be left-handed.

WRITING PRACTICE pages 14–15

Answers vary throughout this section.

JOURNAL

Ask students to write a paragraph about how the facts in the reading fit or do not fit their own personalities based on whether they are left-handed or right-handed.

READING ■ 2
Let's Face It

PRE-READING page 16

Begin the lesson in one of the following ways:

- Draw the five geometric shapes on the board that are mentioned in the reading: *round*, *diamond*, *rectangle*, *square*, and *triangle*. See if students can explain what the different shapes are and see if they can label them correctly. Help them label any they don't know. You may also want to introduce the word "oval" and draw that shape on the board.

- Draw different geometric shapes on the board, label them, and ask students to say what shape face they think they have. Ask other students if they disagree or agree.

- Draw different geometric shapes on the board and label them. Bring in some photos of famous people and ask students to say what shape face they have.

PREPARING FOR THE READING TOPIC
Answers will vary.

KEY VOCABULARY

1. g **3.** e **5.** d **7.** c
2. f **4.** a **6.** h **8.** b

VOCABULARY pages 19–20

VOCABULARY IN CONTEXT

A 1. jaw 5. reliable
2. cheekbones 6. fragile
3. will 7. generous
4. creative 8. confident

B *Answers will vary.*

VOCABULARY BUILDING

1. generosity 4. creativity
2. generous 5. reliable
3. to create 6. rely

Additional Vocabulary Activity

Draw a simple outline of a person's face on the board, including these parts: forehead, eyes, eyebrows, nose, mouth, lips, teeth, ears, cheeks, and chin/jaw. Draw a line from each part and have students take turns labeling the different parts of the face.

READING COMPREHENSION pages 20–21

LOOKING FOR MAIN IDEAS

1. b 2. a 3. b

LOOKING FOR DETAILS

1. The Chinese believe that people with round faces are **confident**.

2. The Chinese believe that it is lucky to meet a person with a **diamond** face before a meeting.

3. The Chinese believe that people with diamond faces are **lucky** in love.

4. The Chinese believe that people with triangular **faces** can get depressed easily.

5. Jacqueline Kennedy had a **wide** jaw and a narrow forehead.

6. Jane Fonda has a wide forehead and **square** chin.

DISCUSSION page 21

Answers will vary.

CRITICAL THINKING page 21

Answers will vary.

WRITING ■ 2

WRITING SKILLS pages 22–25

EXERCISE 1

Some people believe that the shape of a person's face shows the general character of the person. The Chinese believe that there are eight basic shapes of the face, and each shape shows a special character. The shapes are round, diamond, rectangle, square, triangle, narrow forehead and wide jaw, wide forehead and square chin, and wide forehead and high cheekbones. Here is what Chinese people say about these shapes.

Round faces have high and flat cheekbones, flat ears, wide noses, and strong mouths with thin lips. People with round faces are very intelligent, and they prefer to work with their brain instead of their body. People with round faces are confident and usually live a long life.

Many movie stars and famous women have diamond faces. The diamond face is narrow at the top and has a pointed chin. The Chinese believe that it is lucky if you meet a man or a woman with a diamond face before you go to an important meeting. People with this type of face are generally lucky in love and in their jobs. They may not be happy when they are young, but they get what they want later in their lives. People with diamond faces are warm, but they have a strong will.

People with rectangular faces control their feelings, but they are intelligent and creative. These people work hard and are very reliable. Their work is very important to them and comes before everything else, even family. They are not easy to be around when they do not feel free or when they feel bored. Many people with rectangular faces are at their best when they are older.

Square faces usually belong to men, but women can also have them. Men with this kind of face are good at making decisions and keeping to them. They are generous and honest. They put their friends first in everything. Both men and women with square faces are lucky and live a long life.

A wide forehead, high cheekbones, and a pointed chin make a triangular face. People with triangular faces are lively and intelligent and often stand out from others; however, they worry too much and their emotions are fragile, so they can get depressed easily. Because of this, they do better in jobs where they work with people.

The Chinese believe that a person with a wide jaw and narrow forehead is like the earth and changes little. People with this kind of face love success and will almost always get what they want, especially money and all that it brings. A man with this kind of face will not be close to his children, but his children will respect his strength. A woman with this kind of face was Jacqueline Kennedy, who had a strong character even in difficult times.

People with wide foreheads and square chins are intelligent and work hard to get what they want. They can be calm and quiet, or they can be the opposite, too, because they like to get attention. Famous movie stars Jane Fonda have this kind of face; so did Picasso, the painter. They usually have a long life and save their energy for important times in life.

People with wide foreheads and high cheekbones show strong character and a lot of energy. This helps them to be normal again if something bad happens. They know what they like and don't like to change their habits. Nevertheless, they like to live a full life.

EXERCISE 2

2. People with triangular faces may not be tall, but they look tall because of the shape of their face.

3. These people are confident, and they will usually live a long life.

4. Some may be movie stars, or they may work as flight attendants.

5. People with high cheekbones know what they want, and it is hard to make them change their minds.

6. People with this shape of face may often be leaders, but they may also be criminals.

7. They can control their feelings, but they are also intelligent and creative.

8. Square faces usually belong to men, but women can have them, too.

EXERCISE 3

Answers will vary.

EXERCISE 4

Peoples with a wide forehead, and high cheekbones have a face that looks solid, and bony. Famous examples of people with this face are **C**hristopher **C**olumbus, **G**reta **G**arbo, and **A**braham **L**incoln.

WRITING PRACTICE   pages 25–26

Answers vary throughout this section.

JOURNAL

Ask students to write a paragraph that describes their face: their hair, their eyes, their nose, etc., and of course the shape of their face. Be careful, though. Some students may be sensitive about writing about their face. If you feel that may be the case, give them the option of writing about the face of someone they know well or a famous person.

WEAVING IT TOGETHER

TIMED WRITING   page 27

Answers will vary.

SEARCH THE INTERNET   page 27

A Suggested keywords:
- famous left-handers

B Suggested keywords:
- physiognomy
- phrenology

WHAT DO YOU THINK NOW?   page 27

1. Fifteen
2. don't have
3. Right
4. eight

UNIT 2 Food

This unit has readings about two very different types of food. One is about a common everyday food that people eat in many countries every day. The other is about very unusual foods that most people would be very reluctant to eat like insects and snakes. You might want to start the unit by looking at the unit opening picture and then have students think about foods they eat very often and foods that they have heard about that people eat, but have never eaten themselves and would never want to eat.

READING ▪ 1
Live a Little: Eat Potatoes!

PRE-READING page 30

Begin the lesson in one of the following ways:

- Have students call out different ways in which potatoes can be prepared.

- Give students three minutes to jot down every potato item that they have eaten in the past week (french fries, potato chips, baked potato, etc.) and how many times. Add up the total number of servings of potato that students have eaten in the past week and divide by the number of students in the class to get the average number of potato servings students eat in a week. Depending on the demographics of the class, you might want to also ask them to write down the number of pasta servings or rice servings and compare the average per week to the average for potatoes.

- Read the following questions to the class and elicit their answers:
  1. Should you eat potatoes that have green spots? (No. They can make you sick.)
  2. What colors can potatoes be? (They can be red, blue, purple, and yellow.)
  3. Which vitamin do potatoes contain a lot of? (Vitamin C)
  4. Are potatoes fattening? (No. They contain no fat and are only 100 calories.)

PREPARING FOR THE READING TOPIC
Answers will vary.

KEY VOCABULARY

1. b	**3.** h	**5.** a	**7.** f
2. d	**4.** g	**6.** e	**8.** c

VOCABULARY pages 33–34
VOCABULARY IN CONTEXT

A
1. imagine	5. baked
2. poison	6. invented
3. instead	7. dishes
4. disease	8. advantages

B *Answers will vary.*

VOCABULARY BUILDING

1. imaginative	4. invention
2. imagine	5. poisonous
3. inventive	6. poison

READING COMPREHENSION pages 34–35

LOOKING FOR MAIN IDEAS

1. a   **2.** c   **3.** a

LOOKING FOR DETAILS

1. Potatoes grew in **Peru** 7,000 years ago.

2. In the **1500s**, the Spanish brought the potato back to Europe.

3. There is poison in the **leaves** of the potato.

4. A disease killed the **potato** in Ireland in 1845.

5. **Two** million people died of hunger in Ireland.

6. The potato dish of Germany is **potato salad**.

Additional Reading Activity

Have students skim the reading for countries that are mentioned in the reading. Make a list on the board. Call on students to choose a country listed on the board and to explain its significance in the history of the potato.

DISCUSSION page 35

Answers will vary.

CRITICAL THINKING page 35

Answers will vary.

WRITING ■ 1

WRITING SKILLS pages 36–38

EXERCISE 1

1. potatoes   **4.** tea
2. rice   **5.** bread
3. hamburger **6.** corn

EXERCISE 2

1. an important part of our diet

2. an important part in our religion

3. easy to grow

4. the basic food of the Irish

5. popular all over the world

6. an important part of people's diets in Asia

EXERCISE 3

1. a   **3.** a   **5.** b
2. b   **4.** b   **6.** a

EXERCISE 4

Sentences 2, 3, 6, 7, and 8 are good topic sentences.

EXERCISE 5

1. bread

2. an important part of our everyday food

3. In my country, bread is an important part of our everyday food.

4. At the beginning

EXERCISE 6

    The **Incas in S**outh America **grew** potatoes for thousands of years before the **S**panish arrived. The **potato** was the main part of their diet and culture. The **Incas** measured time by how long it took to cook potatoes. They also used potatoes to tell their **f**ortune. If they found an odd number of potatoes, it was bad luck. If they found **an** even number, it was good luck.

Additional Writing Skills Activity

Have students work in pairs and look back at Reading 1 and other readings that they have studied up to now in the book. Ask students to identify at least two excellent and two weak topic sentences from those readings and be prepared to make an argument to the rest of the class why their chosen topic sentences are good or bad.

WRITING PRACTICE   pages 39–40

Answers vary throughout this section.

JOURNAL

Ask students to write about their favorite food and any facts they know about how it is made, how it was discovered, and whether it is healthy or unhealthy.

READING ▪ 2
Bugs, Rats, and Other Tasty Dishes

PRE-READING   page 41

Begin the lesson in one of the following ways:

- Bring to class pictures of unusual foods. See if students can identify them. Ask students whether or not they have eaten them or would like to eat them.

- Ask students to try to draw (have them use colored markers if they are available) unusual foods that are eaten in their cultures. Have other students try to guess what they have drawn. Once the students guess or the student tells the class what it is, ask the class who would be prepared to eat it and why, or why not.

Additional Pre-Reading Activity

Have selected students read out the first sentence of each paragraph. The rest of the students have their books closed. Now ask the class to guess what the whole reading is going to be about.

PREPARING FOR THE READING TOPIC
Answers will vary.

KEY VOCABULARY

1. c	**3.** d	**5.** h	**7.** e
2. f	**4.** a	**6.** g	**8.** b

VOCABULARY   pages 44–45
VOCABULARY IN CONTEXT

A
1. delicacy	**5.** appetizer
2. alive	**6.** native
3. grilled	**7.** dessert
4. pork	**8.** paste

B *Answers will vary.*

VOCABULARY BUILDING

1. a grill	**4.** special
2. grilled	**5.** to live
3. the specialty	**6.** alive

Additional Vocabulary Activity

In the vocabulary activity, students learn the verb "to grill." Ask students to skim through the reading and find any other verbs that describe ways of cooking or preparing food. Students might find: *deep-fry*, *salt*, *dry*, *fry*, and *mash*. Now make two columns on the board: "Ways of Preparing Food" and "Ways of Cooking Food." See how many additional words students can add to each column. Help them find some of the more obvious words. If students gets a chance to do homework before this activity, have them bring in one or two recipes in English and find the verbs that describe food preparation and cooking to add to the lists.

READING COMPREHENSION   pages 45–46
LOOKING FOR MAIN IDEAS

1. b	**2.** a	**3.** c

LOOKING FOR DETAILS

1. T	**3.** F	**5.** F
2. F	**4.** T	**6.** T

DISCUSSION page 46

Answers will vary.

CRITICAL THINKING page 46

Answers will vary.

WRITING ▪ 2

WRITING SKILLS pages 47–50

EXERCISE 1

1. d   **2.** c   **3.** b   **4.** c

EXERCISE 2

Answers will vary.

EXERCISE 3

1. The people in my country make a special dish from the *izote* flower, which is delicious to eat.
2. Nine
3. Some support each other (ex. *To prepare this dish . . .*)
4. Yes. Last sentence.

EXERCISE 4

    We all know that **M**uslims don't eat **pork,** but many people don't know that in **P**akistan they never offer beef to **an** important guest. Beef is cheap and easily available, so a **P**akistani would never offer a guest something as common as steak. Instead, he or she would serve leg of lam**b** as an **appetizer** and chicken, or fish as **a** main course.

> ### Additional Writing Skills Activity
>
> Have students work in pairs and look back at paragraphs 6 and 7 in Reading 2. Ask them to find the topic sentence and the supporting details in these two paragraphs. Have students share their answers with the class.

WRITING PRACTICE pages 50–52

Answers vary throughout this section.

JOURNAL

Ask students to write about an unusual food that they have eaten. Have them write about when and where they ate it, why they ate it, and whether or not they enjoyed it.

WEAVING IT TOGETHER

TIMED WRITING page 53

Answers will vary.

SEARCH THE INTERNET page 53

A Suggested keywords:
- the history of rice
- the history of corn

B Suggested keywords:
- strange delicacies around the world

WHAT DO YOU THINK NOW? page 53

1. Peru/South America
2. were
3. fish heads
4. snakes

UNIT 3 Celebrations and Special Days

The readings in this unit introduce students to two very different types of celebrations from two very different cultures. One is a coming-of-age celebration in Latin America; the other is a Hindu religious festival and celebration that takes place in Nepal, India.

READING ▪ 1
Tihar: Festival of Lights

PRE-READING page 56

Begin the lesson in one of the following ways:

- Bring in photos or draw on the board objects that are connected with various celebrations. For example, you could draw a Christmas tree, a national flag, a wedding ring, a red heart for Valentine's Day, or a cake with candles. Have students guess what celebration the object represents and describe how people in their cultures celebrate this day or something similar.

- Before class, write the names of different holidays or celebrations on small slips of paper. Have enough different holidays so that half of the class gets a different holiday each. Write the holiday name on two pieces of paper. Hand out the slips of paper so that every student gets one. Now have students mingle to find the other student in the class who has the same holiday as them. After the students find each other, have them pool their knowledge of the festival or holiday and report to the class what they know about it.

PREPARING FOR THE READING TOPIC
Answers will vary.

KEY VOCABULARY

1. g	**3.** b	**5.** e	**7.** f
2. h	**4.** a	**6.** d	**8.** c

VOCABULARY pages 59–60
VOCABULARY IN CONTEXT

A
1. worship	**5.** icon
2. holy	**6.** mud
3. please	**7.** trail
4. stray	**8.** prosperity

B *Answers will vary.*

VOCABULARY BUILDING

1. pleasure	**4.** prosperous
2. pleased	**5.** stray
3. prosperity	**6.** stray

READING COMPREHENSION pages 60–61
LOOKING FOR MAIN IDEAS

1. b   **2.** a   **3.** d

LOOKING FOR DETAILS
Possible answers:

1. Hindus celebrate the festival of Tihar in Nepal.

2. People worship crows to keep sadness away.

3. People pray for the dogs to guard their homes.

4. The cow is the symbol of wealth.

5. A female family member performs a special ceremony or *puja*.

6. Brothers honor their sisters by putting garlands around their necks and by giving them gifts of clothes and money.

DISCUSSION page 61

Answers will vary.

> **Additional Discussion Activity**
>
> Before class, have students interview an older relative about how a festival or celebration in their culture was celebrated in the past when they were young. In class, have the students talk about how the celebration used to be celebrated and how it is celebrated today, noting the major differences.

CRITICAL THINKING page 61

Answers will vary.

WRITING ■ 1

WRITING SKILLS pages 62–64

EXERCISE 1

In my country, we call the new year *Tet*. <u>First</u>, on the night the new year begins, we go to the temple. We pray to Buddha, give thanks for the past year, and pray that the new year will be happy. <u>Then</u> we return home. <u>Next</u>, just before midnight, my father bows before an altar we have for our dead relatives. He offers food to the relatives and invites them to join the family. At midnight, we have firecrackers,

and children make a lot of noise. It is Tet. The new year is here. <u>Finally</u>, we sit down and have a big and delicious dinner. We celebrate all night.

EXERCISE 2

1. 2, 1, 4, 3, 6, 5
2. 2, 1, 4, 3
3. 1, 4, 3, 2, 5

EXERCISE 3

1. People worship different animals such as the crow, the dog, and the cow.
2. Tihar takes place in late autumn and lasts for five days. [no comma needed]
3. Tihar is a time to worship animals, brothers and sisters, and the goddess Laxmi.
4. The city is full of lights and decorations. [no comma needed]
5. They put garlands around the animals' necks, give them special food, and make them gifts.
6. Sisters wish their brothers long life and prosperity. [no comma needed]

EXERCISE 4

The Chinese New Year Celebration is 15 days long. The Chinese clean their homes and decorate**, too**. They also buy new clothes and prepare plenty of food. The big celebration start**s** on **N**ew **Y**ear's **E**ve. First, they have a big dinner with plenty of food. There are always special foods like a whole fish**,** chicken**,** and long noodles for long life. After dinner, the whole family sits up for the night. They play games**,** or watch television. Finally**,** there are fireworks all over the sky at midnight.

WRITING PRACTICE pages 65–66

Answers vary throughout this section.

JOURNAL

Ask students to write about their favorite holiday or celebration. What do they usually wear? What do they eat? What do they usually do?

READING ■ 2
Celebrating a Fifteenth Birthday

PRE-READING page 67

Begin the lesson in one of the following ways:

- Make a timeline on the board, marking off ten-year intervals from 0 to 100. Tell students that these numbers represent birthdays between being born and reaching a 100 years of age. Ask students to indicate a number on the timeline that represents a significant birthday in their culture and have them tell you why. You can write the number on the timeline and note the culture or country where that number is significant and write a brief note next to it that explains why it is important. For example, you could write next to the number 18: *The United States—age someone can vote.*

- Write the words "child" and "adult" on the board. Have students work in small groups to discuss the difference between being a child and being an adult. Have students try to reach an agreement on at when you can no longer call a person a child. Have students try to reach an agreement on when you should recognize that someone is an adult. See if they can put an age on these milestones. Have a representative from each group report their discussion back to the class.

PREPARING FOR THE READING TOPIC

Answers will vary.

KEY VOCABULARY

1. b	**3.** f	**5.** c	**7.** h
2. g	**4.** d	**6.** a	**8.** e

VOCABULARY pages 70–71

VOCABULARY IN CONTEXT

A
1. afford	5. blessings
2. godparents	6. proud of
3. bouquet	7. pose
4. guests	8. grown-up

B *Answers will vary.*

VOCABULARY BUILDING

1. blessing	4. affordable
2. to bless	5. grow up
3. afford	6. grown-up

READING COMPREHENSION page 71

LOOKING FOR MAIN IDEAS

1. b	**2.** b	**3.** d

LOOKING FOR DETAILS

1. F	**3.** T	**5.** F
2. T	**4.** F	**6.** T

DISCUSSION page 72

Answers will vary.

CRITICAL THINKING page 72

Answers will vary.

WRITING ■ 2

WRITING SKILLS pages 73–76

EXERCISE 1

2. dependent clause
3. dependent clause
4. main clause
5. dependent clause
6. main clause
7. main clause
8. dependent clause

EXERCISE 2

1. Before they go to the party, they pose for photographs.

2. After they have dinner, there is dancing.

3. They have a church ceremony before they have the special party. [no comma needed]

4. After the church ceremony is over, her parents embrace her.

5. The parents must rent a hall and a band to play music before they have a reception. [no comma needed]

6. The party can begin after the girl and her family arrives at the hall. [no comma needed]

EXERCISE 3

2. Before they go to the party, the girl and her attendants pose for photographs.

3. After the guests have dinner, the girl starts to dance with her father.

4. After the girl dances with her father, the other guests dance.

EXERCISE 4

Last year, my oldest brother got married. His bride was his friend's sister. First, they had a civil marriage in the town hall. A few weeks later, they had a church wedding. The bride wore a beautiful white dress and a veil over her face. The bridegroom wore a tuxedo. After the religious ceremony was over, the newlyweds and the guests went to a restaurant near the church. Here there was a wonderful wedding reception with all kinds of hot and cold food. After that, there was music and dancing. Before the reception ended, the bride and groom met and thanked every guest. Finally, after the reception was over, the newlyweds went on a trip to Hawaii for their honeymoon.

EXERCISE 5

First, you need to invite your closest relatives, like parents, grandparents, aunts, uncles, godparents, brothers, sisters, and close friends. Then, you must decide what food you will give your guests at the dinner. Next, you must pick out a church and a hall. Finally, you must pick out a dress. For many girls, this is the **most important** thing.

WRITING PRACTICE pages 76–78

Answers vary throughout this section.

JOURNAL

Ask students to write a paragraph about their favorite birthday. What happened on that birthday? What made it so special?

WEAVING IT TOGETHER

TIMED WRITING page 79

Answers will vary.

SEARCH THE INTERNET page 79

A Suggested keywords:
- día del amor y la amistad
- Kodomo no hi
- N'cwala

B Suggested keywords:
- coming-of-age around the world
- important birthdays in different countries

WHAT DO YOU THINK NOW? page 79

1. small country
2. is
3. is not
4. fifteenth

UNIT 4 Amazing People

The readings in this unit introduce students to two amazing men. Both are adventurers who have traveled all over the world. One found excitement through flying airplanes and introducing others to flying. The other man also found adventure in heights, but he did not fly to those heights. Instead, he climbed mountains and walked in some of the world's most dangerous places. You can introduce students to the unit by looking at the unit opener photo. Ask students to try to understand the photo and have them think about how people can find adventure in high places.

READING ■ 1
Barrington Irving's Dream to Fly

PRE-READING page 82

Begin the lesson in one of the following ways:

- Bring to class photos of different types of aircraft. Find photos that range from early aircraft up to the space shuttle. Try to include planes from different eras and ask students to try to identify the types of planes and the eras that they come from. Ask students to tell you which aircraft they would like to fly in and which they would not and why.

- Have students look at the photo of Barrington Irving on pages 82–83. Ask them how they would describe him: his age, his ethnicity, the expression on his face, and his personality. Then ask them to describe the plane behind him. Have them predict from the photo and the title of the reading what the reading might be about.

PREPARING FOR THE READING TOPIC
Answers will vary.

KEY VOCABULARY

1. g	**3.** a	**5.** b	**7.** c
2. d	**4.** f	**6.** h	**8.** e

VOCABULARY pages 84–86

VOCABULARY IN CONTEXT

A
1. solo	**5.** solve problems
2. neighborhoods	**6.** license
3. careers	**7.** determined
4. limit	**8.** equipment

B *Answers will vary.*

VOCABULARY BUILDING

1. determine	**4.** equip
2. determined	**5.** limited
3. equipment	**6.** limit

Additional Vocabulary Activity

Draw a simple plane on the board, showing two pilots sitting next to each other and passengers and arrows showing the plane going up and the plane coming down. Draw lines to your drawing so that you can elicit from students the following vocabulary: *wing, pilot, co-pilot, cockpit, engine, passenger, take off,* and *land*.

READING COMPREHENSION pages 86–87

LOOKING FOR MAIN IDEAS

1. c **2.** a **3.** d

LOOKING FOR DETAILS

1. Irving was born in **Jamaica** in 1983.

2. While Irving was working at **a bookstore**, he met an airline pilot who took him on a short flight.

3. When Irving was in college, he wanted to **share his love of flying with** high school students in poor neighborhoods.

4. Some airplane makers **gave** Irving parts so he could build his own plane.

5. When Irving taught some young people how to put a plane together, he also helped them to **understand math and science**.

6. While Irving was making his solo flight around the world, students all over the world followed his flight **on the Internet**.

Additional Reading Activity

Have students scan the reading for significant dates and ages in Barrington's life. Have students translate the ages into dates so that they can make a timeline for Barrington Irving's life and achievements. For example, we read that he was born in 1983 and moved to Miami when he was six. Therefore, they can put "1989" for the year he moved to Miami.

DISCUSSION page 87

Answers will vary.

CRITICAL THINKING page 87

Answers will vary.

WRITING ▪ 1

WRITING SKILLS pages 88–90

EXERCISE 1

(My sister Liz) was born lucky. She has a beautiful smile. *1* When she does something bad, she smiles and my parents are not angry. *2* She eats a lot and does not get fat. Her favorite meal is a double cheeseburger with french fries, a milkshake, and an ice cream sundae. *3* She does not study hard but always gets good grades. After school, she does her homework in five minutes while she watches television at the same time. In conclusion, I believe that some people are born lucky, and some are not.

5. *Answers will vary.*

EXERCISE 2

1. Cheng has not been lucky in school this year. He got sick and missed classes and could not take his finals. He also lost his books. These were not only his textbooks but also his notebooks. Everybody likes Cheng because he will go out of his way to help people.

2. My roommate Tony is very untidy. He has brown hair and blue eyes. He leaves his laundry on the floor. When he cooks, he never washes the dishes. For a while, he had a bicycle on his bed. It is not surprising that Tony can never find anything.

3. Uncle Santiago is very clumsy. When he drinks coffee, he always spills some on his shirt. In the shopping mall, he walks into other people all the time. He has size 14 feet. Last time he came to our house, he sat on the cat.

4. Aunt Dotty loves adventure. On her 60th birthday, she went mountain climbing in the Alps. On her 70th birthday, she went on a trip to the North Pole. When she was 80, she drove solo across the United States. <u>She loves to eat chocolate.</u> We all wonder what she will do when she is 90.

EXERCISE 3

Amelia **E**arhart was born in **K**ansas, USA, in 1897. She was the **f**irst woman to fly solo across the **A**tlantic Ocean. Earhart also became the **f**irst woman to fly from **C**alifornia to **H**awaii. In 1937, Earhart wanted to fly around the world. She start**ed** her **flight**, but she and her **plane** were never found.

WRITING PRACTICE pages 90–92

Answers vary throughout this section.

JOURNAL

Ask students to write about a flight that they have taken that was particularly interesting or exciting. If they have not flown, they can write about a famous flight that they know about.

READING ■ 2
The Fearless Fiennes

PRE-READING page 93

Begin the lesson in one of the following ways:

- Have students name famous mountains and mountain ranges in the world. Ask them if they know where they are and how high they are.

- Find out how much students know about the differences between the Arctic and the Antarctic.

- Ask students to discuss marathon running. Have they ever run one? Would they like to run one? Do they know how many miles or kilometers a marathon is? Do they know what training is needed to run a marathon?

PREPARING FOR THE READING TOPIC
Answers will vary.

KEY VOCABULARY

1. c	**3.** a	**5.** d	**7.** e
2. h	**4.** f	**6.** b	**8.** g

VOCABULARY pages 96–97
VOCABULARY IN CONTEXT

A 1. reach
2. get rid of
3. records
4. surgery
5. charities
6. extreme
7. give up
8. raise money

B *Answers will vary.*

VOCABULARY BUILDING

A 1. raise your voice
2. raise money
3. raise hopes

B *Answers will vary.*

READING COMPREHENSION pages 97–98
LOOKING FOR MAIN IDEAS

1. b   2. d   3. c

LOOKING FOR DETAILS
Possible answers:

1. Fiennes and Burton crossed the Arctic Ocean.

2. *The Transglobe Expedition* took three years and covered 52,000 miles.

3. Fiennes found the lost city of Ubar in 1992 in Oman.

4. Fiennes couldn't complete his North Pole expedition in 2000 because his sled fell through the ice.

5. After his heart surgery, Fiennes had to learn how to walk again.

6. Fiennes tried to cross the Antarctica in winter during the *The Coldest Journey* expedition.

Additional Reading Activity

Bring copies of a map of the world for each student in the class or have students draw a crude map of the world on a piece of paper. Then have students scan through the reading and identify the different places mentioned in the reading on the map.

DISCUSSION   page 98

Answers will vary.

Additional Discussion Activity

Write the different achievements of Ranulph Fiennes on the board. Have students help you make the list. Put students in groups and have them discuss which of Ranulph's achievements was the most impressive and which the least impressive. Ask students to come to a consensus and put all Ranulph's achievements in rank order from most to least impressive.

CRITICAL THINKING   page 98

Answers will vary.

WRITING ▪ 2

WRITING SKILLS   pages 99–101

EXERCISE 1

My brother is very selfish. He does not want to share things with other people. (For example), when he buys a chocolate bar, he puts it in a secret place. Then he eats it all, by himself. He never helps anyone. He says he is busy. (For example), a game on the computer makes him very busy. He does not care if something he does bothers other people. (For instance), last night he played loud rock 'n' roll music until four o'clock in the morning. In conclusion, I think my brother is selfish and will always be selfish.

1. For example; For instance
2. yes
3. yes
4. yes

EXERCISE 2

Possible answers:

1. For example**,** he gets food all over his shirt.

2. For instance, **she never** washes **the** dishes.

3. For example**,** she always wants me to do things for her.

4. For instance, **she is** a doctor.

5. For instance**,** she always leaves the bathroom in a mess.

6. For example, **he went** to the North Pole.

EXERCISE 3

Answers will vary.

EXERCISE 4

Answers will vary.

EXERCISE 5

     Howard **H**ughes was born in **T**exas in 1906. He was one of the richest men in the world**,** but he was very strange. For example**,** he **ate** the same dinner every night: a steak**,** a potato**,** and 12 peas. Later in his life, he became even stranger. For instance**,** he did not wear clothes and did not cut his **hair**. Hughes **died** without any friends in 1976.

WRITING PRACTICE   pages 102–104

Answers vary throughout this section.

JOURNAL

Explain what it means to "overcome obstacles." Ask students to write about an achievement in their lives in which they had to overcome obstacles.

WEAVING IT TOGETHER

TIMED WRITING   page 105

Answers will vary.

SEARCH THE INTERNET   page 105

A Suggested keywords:
- Will Steger
- Conrad Anker
- Børge Ousland

B Suggested keywords:
- Edmund Hillary

WHAT DO YOU THINK NOW?   page 105

1. is
2. can
3. can
4. is not

UNIT 5 Nature Attacks!

In this unit, students read about two natural phenomena that can be deadly. The first reading gives many facts about lightning. The second is a more personal story that has a tragic ending.

READING ■ 1
Lightning

PRE-READING page 108

Begin the lesson in one of the following ways:

- Rub a balloon on a piece of fabric and place the side you rubbed against the wall. The balloon will stick to the wall. See if a student can explain why this happens or explain that the negative charges on the balloon and the positive charges on the wall attract each other. In the same way, the negative charge on a cloud is attracted to the positive charge on the surface of the earth. However, instead of the cloud and the earth moving toward each other, the electricity jumps from the cloud to the earth. Use a simple drawing on the board to illustrate the lightning bolt.

- Write the word "lightning" on the board, and then draw a chart with three columns. Add the headings "Things I am sure about," "Things I am not sure about," and "Things I don't know." Have students call out facts or uncertainties about lightning and assign them to one of the three columns.

PREPARING FOR THE READING TOPIC

Answers will vary.

KEY VOCABULARY

1. b	**3.** h	**5.** e	**7.** f
2. g	**4.** d	**6.** c	**8.** a

VOCABULARY pages 111–112
VOCABULARY IN CONTEXT

A
1. lightning bolts	**5.** exploding
2. amaze	**6.** protect
3. frighten	**7.** shelter
4. injured	**8.** attract

B *Answers will vary.*

VOCABULARY BUILDING

1. amazing	**4.** frightening
2. amazement	**5.** attractive
3. fright	**6.** attraction

READING COMPREHENSION pages 112–113
LOOKING FOR MAIN IDEAS

1. c   **2.** a   **3.** c

LOOKING FOR DETAILS
Possible answers:

1. Every year about 100 people die from lightning in the United States and Canada.

2. We see lightning first because light travels almost a million times faster than sound.

3. Metal attracts lightning very quickly.

4. The Empire State Building in New York City gets hit by lightning 25 times a year.

5. Benjamin Franklin invented the lightning rod in 1750.

6. Roy Sullivan was hit by lightning seven times in his life.

Additional Reading Activity

Remind students that they learned that paragraphs should have topics. Have students work in pairs to decide what the topics of the body paragraphs (2–5) are in this reading. Then open the discussion up to the whole class. Possible answers:

Paragraph 2: the power of lightning

Paragraph 3: the speed of lightning

Paragraph 4: protecting tall buildings from lightning

Paragraph 5: what to do when you see lightning

DISCUSSION page 113

Answers will vary.

CRITICAL THINKING page 113

Answers will vary.

WRITING ▪ 1

WRITING SKILLS pages 114–115

EXERCISE 1

1. <u>October 1, 1987, was a frightening day for me.</u>

2. October 1, 1987. Suddenly, the room started to shake. Some dishes fell to the floor. I got under a table. 7:30 on a Thursday morning.

3. I came out and tried to turn on the television. A few minutes later.

4. I tried the telephone. After that. The neighbors came to see if I was all right. Shortly after.

5. My mother called me. Finally, at about 9:00 a.m.

EXERCISE 2

1. The San Francisco earthquake hit on the morning of April 18, 1906.

2. On December 26, 2004, a tsunami hit Asia.

3. The biggest earthquake recorded in North America was the earthquake on March 27, 1964.

4. Suddenly, people heard a noise like thunder.

5. A terrible earthquake hit Kobe, Japan, in 1995.

6. A tsunami hit Sumatra, Indonesia, after the earthquake.

7. A few minutes later, buildings washed away.

8. Shortly after, a tsunami hit the coast of Sri Lanka.

EXERCISE 3

In the United States, the **s**tates with the greatest number of deaths from lightning are Florida, **T**exas, and **N**orth Carolina. Avoid these states, especially in June, which is the worst month for lightning. The other bad months are **A**ugust, **J**uly, **A**pril, and September.

Ask students to write sentences that begin "I was born . . ." Tell them to use the correct prepositions and commas (if needed). Each sentence will provide the following information about the students. If the first and last sentences (see below) might embarrass some students, you can avoid them or use them as examples with a student you don't think will be embarrassed. Alternatively, give example sentences about yourself if you won't be embarrassed.

For example, the first sentence might be: *I was born in 1994.*

> The year of their birth
> The month of their birth
> The day of the week of their birth
> The exact time of their birth
> The time of day of their birth
> The city and country of their birth
> The date of their birth

WRITING PRACTICE pages 116–117

Answers vary throughout this section.

JOURNAL

Ask students to describe any experiences they have had with lightning. Have them write about the weather at the time of the lightning, the closeness of the lightning, and whether there was thunder. Did the lightning hit anything?

READING ▪ 2
Chasing Storms

PRE-READING page 118

Begin the lesson in one of the following ways:

• Write the following words on the board: *rain*, *snow*, *hail*, *ice*, *thunder*, *dust*, and *sand*. Tell students that each word can go together with the word *storm*, for example, *snowstorm* or *dust storm*. See if students can tell you about each type of storm. See if they can tell you where and at what time of year they might occur.

• Have students look at the photo on pages 106–107 and read the caption. Ask them what they know about tornados. Ask students what they would do if they knew that a tornado was near where they were. Now have them look at the photo on pages 118–119 and have them read the title of the reading. Ask them to predict what the man in the picture would do.

• Explain the expressions "to be daring" and "to take risks." Ask students to tell you about people who do daring things and who take risks.

PREPARING FOR THE READING TOPIC
Answers will vary.

KEY VOCABULARY

1. h	**3.** g	**5.** e	**7.** d
2. f	**4.** c	**6.** b	**8.** a

VOCABULARY pages 121–122
VOCABULARY IN CONTEXT

A
1. destroy		**5.** focus
2. forecasts		**6.** develop
3. brilliant		**7.** flat
4. twist		**8.** path

B *Answers will vary.*

VOCABULARY BUILDING

1. to focus
2. focus
3. twist
4. to twist
5. to destroy
6. destructive

READING COMPREHENSION pages 122–123

LOOKING FOR MAIN IDEAS

1. a   2. d   3. b

LOOKING FOR DETAILS

1. T   3. T   5. F
2. F   4. T   6. F

DISCUSSION page 123

Answers will vary.

CRITICAL THINKING page 123

Answers will vary.

Additional Critical Thinking Activity

Ask students to think about different reasons that people take risks. Help elicit such answers as: *to get excitement, to save someone's life, to learn things about the world that were previously unknown,* and *to go to places that have never been explored before.* (If you do the additional Critical Thinking activity after you study the Writing Skills section, you can ask students to use "because" in their answers.)

Once you have elicited some reasons, you can ask students to think about what motivated Tim Samaras. Then have students come up with other people who died while doing something risky. Ask students to think about what reason or reasons motivated them.

WRITING ▪ 2

WRITING SKILLS pages 124–126

EXERCISE 1

1. Hurricanes are huge storms with strong winds and rain, and they are a major problem where I live.

2. Global warming is making hurricanes happen more often. / Hurricanes are becoming more powerful. / Because of changes in weather patterns, hurricanes are lasting longer.

3. First; Second; Third

4. Yes

5. Because of the danger of flooding in the next hurricane, his parents want to move somewhere safer.

EXERCISE 2

2. There are a lot of tornadoes in the central part of the United States because the land is flat and the air conditions create powerful thunderstorms. / Because the land is flat and the air conditions create powerful thunderstorms, there are a lot of tornadoes in the central part of the United States.

3. Samaras created special equipment because he wanted to learn important information about tornadoes. / Because he wanted to learn important information about tornadoes, Samaras created special equipment.

4. Tornadoes are very dangerous because they have powerful winds that twist into a funnel shape and pick things up from the ground. / Because they have powerful winds that twist into a funnel shape and pick things up from the ground, tornadoes are very dangerous.

EXERCISE 3

Even small thunderstorms are **d**angerous. The reason **is** that every thunderstorm produces lightning. **Did** you know that lightning kill**s** and injures more **people** each year than hurricanes or tornados**?** Where there is thunder, there is lightning. If you **hear** thunder, go indoors or **get** in a car. A car **is** a safe place to be. It is **not** safe outside where lightning can strike you.

WRITING PRACTICE   pages 127–128

Answers vary throughout this section.

JOURNAL

Ask students to write about the riskiest or most dangerous thing that they have ever done. Ask them to write about why they did it and what happened.

WEAVING IT TOGETHER

TIMED WRITING   page 129

Answers will vary.

SEARCH THE INTERNET   page 129

A Suggested keywords:
- preparing for a hurricane / tornado / flood / earthquake / volcanic eruption
- city emergency disaster plans

B Suggested keywords:
- recent natural disasters in the world

WHAT DO YOU THINK NOW?   page 129

1. die
2. is not
3. don't know
4. has

UNIT 6 Inventions

The readings in this unit describe two different innovations in technology. The first reading is about a piece of technological hardware that can create exciting video images. The second reading describes advances in biotechnology.

You may want to get students into the unit theme by having them look at the unit opener photo on pages 130–131 Ask them to be creative and to think about what robotic fish might be used for. There are many possible answers: Some robotic fish are put in the ocean to detect degrees of ocean pollution; other robotic fish are simply used to be entertaining and put in aquariums; future uses might be in search and rescue, the fishing industry, and of course the military. See how many different ideas students can come up with.

READING ■ 1
The GoPro Camera

PRE-READING page 132

Begin the lesson in one of the following ways:

- Bring in photos of different pieces of personal technology, such as laptops, phones, and MP3 players, etc. Ask students to tell you what their favorite piece of technology is and why.

- Have students look at the photo on pages 132–133. Ask them to think of other "high thrill" sports. Ask students to tell you where they could place a video camera on a piece of equipment of the person doing the sport or on the person doing the sport to be able to make a great video. Have they seen such video? What did it look like?

PREPARING FOR THE READING TOPIC

Answers will vary.

KEY VOCABULARY

1. f	**3.** a	**5.** b	**7.** c
2. h	**4.** e	**6.** g	**8.** d

VOCABULARY pages 135–136

VOCABULARY IN CONTEXT

A
1. training	**5.** disappointed
2. attach	**6.** vehicle
3. at least	**7.** memorable
4. shared	**8.** evidence

B *Answers will vary.*

VOCABULARY BUILDING

1. memory	**4.** an attachment
2. to memorize	**5.** to disappoint
3. to attach	**6.** disappointment

READING COMPREHENSION pages 136–137

LOOKING FOR MAIN IDEAS

1. a	**2.** d	**3.** d

LOOKING FOR DETAILS

1. The GoPro camera is small and **easy** to carry.

2. Woodman didn't start to develop his camera until after he went to **Australia**.

3. Woodman thought that at least some **surfers** would be happy with a wearable camera.

4. Woodman and his girlfriend made money by selling **belts**.

5. In **its first full year** of sales, GoPro made $350,000.

6. Athletes use the GoPro **for training**.

DISCUSSION page 137

Answers will vary.

CRITICAL THINKING page 137

Answers will vary.

WRITING ▪ 1

WRITING SKILLS pages 138–140

EXERCISE 1

1. I got a smart phone for my birthday, and I soon realized what a useful invention this is.

2. Someone can get in touch with me wherever I am. They can leave me a voice message, text message, or email. Now I can take a photo or video of it. I do not need to take a camera with me. It is easy to carry in my pocket.

3. and 4.

I got a smart phone for my birthday, and I soon realized what a useful invention this is. I travel a lot, so now

someone can get in touch with me wherever I am. If I am busy, they can leave me a voice message, text message, or email message, and I can get back to them. It doesn't matter where I am. Sometimes when I am traveling, I see something I want to remember. Now I can take a photo or video of it because my new phone has a camera in it. Therefore, I do not need to take a camera with me. It is also very small and light, so it is easy to carry in my pocket. In conclusion, I really do not know how I lived without this wonderful invention.

EXERCISE 2

1. Mr. Kim has a hearing problem; therefore, he wears a hearing aid.

2. Janet does not like to wear her glasses, so she is wearing contact lenses.

3. Peter bought an expensive car. Therefore, he had to get a car alarm.

4. Jose got a photocopier for his office, so he does not have to go to the copy store every day.

5. Kathy always has her cell phone with her; therefore, you can contact her at any time.

6. Tony hates to wash dishes, so he bought a dishwasher.

EXERCISE 3

1. c	**3.** e	**5.** d
2. b	**4.** a	

EXERCISE 4

2. a. C **b.** E

Possible answer: Because I forgot to put batteries in it, my portable radio does not work.

3. a. E   **b.** C

Possible answer: There is a snowstorm in Canada, so the flight from Canada is three hours late.

4. a. C   **b.** E

Possible answer: I cannot see well with these old glasses, so I need to have my eyes tested again.

EXERCISE 5

Two students from Stanford University in **California started** a project **in** 1996. They created a search engine. They called **it** Google. It **became** very **popular**. People started to use the verb *to google* when **they** wanted to look up something **on** the Internet. Today, the verb *google* is in the **d**ictionary.

Additional Writing Skills Activity

Put students in pairs and have them create a chain of events in which one event causes another event that causes another event and so on. Give them an example.

> I woke up late so I missed my train. / I missed my train; therefore, I arrived late at work. / I arrived late at work, so my boss was very angry, etc.

Here are some possible ideas to begin each chain:

> Someone stole my computer.
> My cell phone broke.
> I put a photo of myself on the Internet.
> I bought a hybrid car.

You can no doubt think of other events that are related to technology to start the chain of effects.

Ask students to come up with a chain of at least four effects. Have them write their chains using *so* and *therefore* in their sentences. Go around the class checking for correct punctuation. Ask selected students to read their chains to the class.

WRITING PRACTICE pages 140–142

Answers vary throughout this section.

JOURNAL

Ask students to write about a piece of technology in their lives that they could not live without. Ask them to imagine how their lives would be different if it had never been invented.

READING ▪ 2
Changing Living Things?

PRE-READING page 143

Begin the lesson in one of the following ways:

- Ask students if they know what the prefix *bio* means. Then ask them to tell you what they think *biotechnology* is. See how much students know about the topic.

- Ask students whether they think it would be a good thing if biotechnology made it possible for humans to live much longer lives. What problems might that create and how might those problems be solved?

- Ask students if they know of any biotechnological advances that have made a difference in their lives? What world problems could biotechnology alleviate in the future?

PREPARING FOR THE READING TOPIC
Answers will vary.

KEY VOCABULARY

1. c	**3.** a	**5.** d	**7.** b
2. g	**4.** e	**6.** h	**8.** f

VOCABULARY pages 146–147

VOCABULARY IN CONTEXT

A
1. crops
2. wrapped
3. peel
4. cell
5. genes
6. insecticides
7. spills
8. resistant

B *Answers will vary.*

VOCABULARY BUILDING

1. resistant
2. resistance
3. peel
4. peel
5. spill
6. spill

READING COMPREHENSION pages 147–148

LOOKING FOR MAIN IDEAS

1. d   2. b   3. d

LOOKING FOR DETAILS

1. T   3. T   5. T
2. F   4. T   6. T

DISCUSSION page 148

Answers will vary.

CRITICAL THINKING page 148

Answers will vary.

WRITING ■ 2

WRITING SKILLS pages 149–152

EXERCISE 1

1. O   3. F   5. O
2. O   4. F

EXERCISE 2

1. Biotechnology creates new animals, plants, and foods. In addition, biotechnology provides us with new medicines and materials.

2. Scientists in the 1960s made corn, wheat, and rice that grew faster and bigger. Moreover, scientists made these crops more resistant to disease and insects.

3. Today, American farmers can grow more crops. In addition, American farmers do not need to use so many insecticides.

4. Tomatoes that have had their genes changed are red and have a perfect shape. Moreover, these tomatoes stay fresh longer.

5. Scientists have created cattle that have more meat. In addition, scientists have created pigs that help people with heart transplants.

6. Using biotechnology, scientists have created microbes that can break up oil. Moreover, scientists have created a plant that takes arsenic from the ground.

EXERCISE 3

1. In my opinion, we get some advantages if we use biotechnology for our food.

2. Advantages: Biotechnology will help to create more food for everybody. New crops will not need insecticides. This will be better for our health. We will have better fruits and vegetables. Disadvantages: The writer doesn't include any.

3. First of all; Second; In addition

4. Today, we have watermelon and grapes with no seeds.

5. In conclusion, biotechnology for our food will give us more food, the food will be better for our health, and we will have better fruits and vegetables.

EXERCISE 4

China is a large country with many people to feed. In the future, China needs even more food. In the past, the **Chinese** government **did** not allow plants that had their genes changed. Today, however**,** **Chinese** scientists are **working** hard to change the genes of rice. They want to create rice that grows in cold temperatures**,**

high places**,** and dry soil. In addition**,** they want **rice** that has **many / a lot of** vitamins and resists insects.

WRITING PRACTICE pages 152–154
Answers vary throughout this section.

JOURNAL

Ask students to take a position on the benefits or problems of biotechnology and write why they hold their opinion. If you did the debate activity with students, they will be well prepared to write this journal entry.

WEAVING IT TOGETHER

TIMED WRITING page 155
Answers will vary.

SEARCH THE INTERNET page 155

A Suggested keywords:
  • the history of Facebook
  • the history of Twitter

B Suggested keywords:
  • biotechnology in agriculture

WHAT DO YOU THINK NOW? page 155

1. difficult
2. can
3. pig
4. can

UNIT 7 Customs and Traditions

The readings in this unit are about traditions and how they vary between cultures. Reading 1 discusses wedding customs, and Reading 2 discusses naming and naming traditions.

READING ▪ 1
Flowers, Dishes, and Dresses

PRE-READING page 158

Begin the lesson in one of the following ways:

- Bring in to class, or have students bring in, pictures of brides and grooms. Pin them up along the walls. Have students guess which country the bride and groom are from. Have students tell the class what clues they used to make their guess.

- Ask student volunteers to describe a wedding that they have been to. What was the bride wearing? What was the groom wearing? What happened during the wedding ceremony? What happened after the wedding ceremony? Have students tell you if this wedding was typical of weddings in their cultures. Have them tell you what was similar and what was different.

- Have students look at the photo on pages 158–159. Who is getting married in this picture? In what ways is this wedding similar to or different from weddings in students' cultures?

PREPARING FOR THE READING TOPIC
Answers will vary.

KEY VOCABULARY

1. h	**3.** d	**5.** e	**7.** f
2. a	**4.** g	**6.** b	**8.** c

VOCABULARY pages 161–162

VOCABULARY IN CONTEXT

A
1. bride	**5.** charms
2. groom	**6.** symbols
3. aisle	**7.** informal
4. crown	**8.** faithfulness

B *Answers will vary.*

VOCABULARY BUILDING

1. symbol	**4.** charming
2. symbolic	**5.** faithful
3. charm	**6.** faithfully

READING COMPREHENSION pages 162–163

LOOKING FOR MAIN IDEAS

1. d	**2.** b	**3.** c

LOOKING FOR DETAILS

1. T	**3.** F	**5.** F
2. F	**4.** T	**6.** T

DISCUSSION   page 163

Answers will vary.

CRITICAL THINKING   page 163

Answers will vary.

WRITING ▪ 1

WRITING SKILLS   pages 164–167

EXERCISE 1

1. The Hindu bride wears red clothes. However, a Japanese bride wears white.

   The Hindu bride wears red clothes; however, a Japanese bride wears white.

2. Some brides in England wear a penny in their shoe. However, in Sweden, the bride puts a gold coin in her right shoe and a silver coin in her left.

   Some brides in England wear a penny in their shoe; however, in Sweden, the bride puts a gold coin in her right shoe and a silver coin in her left.

3. In Finland, it is traditional for a bride to wear a crown. However, in the United States, the bride usually wears a veil.

   In Finland, it is traditional for a bride to wear a crown; however, in the United States, the bride usually wears a veil.

4. In Turkey, if you catch a candy that the bride throws, you will wed soon. However, in the United States, you will marry soon if you catch the bride's bouquet.

   In Turkey, if you catch a candy that the bride throws, you will wed soon; however, in the United States, you will marry soon if you catch the bride's bouquet.

EXERCISE 2

1. In Nepal, red powder on a woman's forehead shows that she is married. Similarly / Likewise, an American woman wears a ring on her left hand.

2. In India, some marriages are arranged. Similarly / Likewise, in Afghanistan, fathers often arrange their sons' and daughters' marriages.

3. In China, friends and guests play jokes on the couple. Similarly / Likewise, in Saudi Arabia, a groom's friends often play jokes on him.

4. In France, the newlyweds drink wine from a traditional wedding cup. Similarly / Likewise, in Japan, a couple drinks rice wine from a small cup.

EXERCISE 3

1. Plan B
2. Brides wear white dresses and veils. The reception can be a sit-down meal.
3. Similarly; Likewise
4. The groom's clothing. The amount of food on the table. The time a reception ends.

5. However

6. Yes

EXERCISE 4

Many countries have a wedding cake tradition. The bride and groom together cut a **piece** of the wedding cake. **The** groom feeds the cake to the bride. Then the bride **feeds** the cake to the groom. Everyone claps and **cheers**. This **tradition** of the cake is symbolic. It is a **symbol** that the couple **has** started to take care of each other. However**,** at some **weddings** today, the bride and groom put the cake in each others' **faces**!

Additional Writing Skills Activity

Have students look back at Exercise 1 (page 165) and Exercise 2 (page 166). Have them choose one of the cultures or countries mentioned in each exercise item and compare or contrast their culture to that of the culture or country mentioned in the item. For example, an American student might answer for item 1 of Exercise 1:

A Japanese bride wears white. Similarly, brides in the United States wear white.

Have students write down their answers, and as they do so, move around the class. Check their work and help students as necessary.

WRITING PRACTICE pages 168–169

Answers vary throughout this section.

JOURNAL

Ask students to write about a wedding that they have attended. Have them describe the bride and groom, the ceremony, and any celebration after or before the ceremony.

READING ■ 2
What's in a Name?

PRE-READING page 170

Begin the lesson in one of the following ways:

- Write on the board some common last names in English. Ask students to guess what the origin of these last names might be:

Smith	Jackson
Taylor	Wright
Baker	Miller
Johnson	Moore
Walker	Wilson
Cook	Hill

- Ask students to share any naming traditions in their culture.

PREPARING FOR THE READING TOPIC
Answers will vary.

KEY VOCABULARY

1. h	**3.** b	**5.** f	**7.** g
2. d	**4.** e	**6.** c	**8.** a

Additional Pre-reading Activity

Write the three questions below on the board. Have students skim the reading to find the answers. Make it into a competition. As each student finds the answers, have each student raise his or her hand and close their book. Once all students have found the answers, ask the first student to raise his or her hand to give the answers.

1. In what countries do people not use last names?

2. In what countries do children keep both their mother's and their father's last names?

3. In what countries does the family name (the last name) come first?

VOCABULARY pages 173–174

VOCABULARY IN CONTEXT

A
1. characteristics
2. landmark
3. abbreviation
4. initial
5. honor
6. paperwork
7. trademark
8. occupations

B *Answers will vary.*

VOCABULARY BUILDING

1. abbreviation
2. abbreviated
3. to occupy
4. occupation
5. honor
6. to honor

READING COMPREHENSION pages 174–175

LOOKING FOR MAIN IDEAS

1. a   2. b   3. d

LOOKING FOR DETAILS

1. Today, Icelanders usually do not use **last** names.

2. **Smith** is the most common name in English-speaking countries.

3. In Scotland, the word *Mac* means **son**.

4. In Spanish-speaking countries, people put their mother's family name **last**.

5. Most people use an initial for their **middle** name.

6. You cannot change your name to a famous **trademark's** name.

DISCUSSION page 175

Answers will vary.

CRITICAL THINKING page 175

Answers will vary.

WRITING ▪ 2

WRITING SKILLS pages 176–177

EXERCISE 1

1. It states the purpose of the letter.
2. It gives supporting information. Yes, it is.
3. Yes, it does.

EXERCISE 2

As you **know**, we can address a woman as *Miss*, *Ms.*, or *Mrs*. If a woman is married, we address her as *Mrs*. If we don't know if a woman is married, we address her as *Ms*. If she is very young, we address her as *Miss*. However**,** men do not have this **d**istinction. We address a man as *Mr.* if he is married or not, young or old.

WRITING PRACTICE page 178

Answers vary throughout this section.

JOURNAL

Ask students to write about their name. Do they like their name? Does it have a special meaning for their family? If they could change their name, what would they change it to, and why?

WEAVING IT TOGETHER

TIMED WRITING   <small>page 179</small>

Answers will vary.

SEARCH THE INTERNET   <small>page 179</small>

A Suggested keywords:
- origin of the name [+ last name]
- meaning of the name [+ first name]

B Suggested keywords:
- most common name in [+ country]

WHAT DO YOU THINK NOW?   <small>page 179</small>

1. don't wear
2. see

3. is not
4. have

UNIT 8 Readings from Literature

In this unit, students read a poem and a short story. Find out if your students like to read poems and short stories. Ask them who their favorite poets or writers are. Ask if they have read something recently that they have enjoyed. Have them describe what it was and why they enjoyed it.

READING ■ 1
Months

PRE-READING page 182

Begin the lesson in one of the following ways:

• See if students know the names of the twelve months of the year and the four seasons in English. Ask them what their favorite month is and why.

• Ask students to name some characteristics of poetry. List their responses on the board. Students may suggest such elements as rhyming words at the ends of lines and repeated rhythmic patterns. Bring into class some short simple poems and ask students to identify some of the characteristics that they mention.

• Have students close their books and play the audio track of the poem on page 183 or read it to the students. Then have them look at the poem as you play the track again or read it to them again. Ask students to respond to the poem. What did they like, or not like, about it?

PREPARING FOR THE READING TOPIC
Answers will vary.

KEY VOCABULARY

1. f	**3.** g	**5.** h	**7.** e
2. d	**4.** a	**6.** c	**8.** b

VOCABULARY pages 184–185

VOCABULARY IN CONTEXT

A
1. in tune		**5.** shoot
2. bears		**6.** torn
3. dripping wet		**7.** bleak
4. rough		**8.** rages

B *Answers will vary.*

VOCABULARY BUILDING

1. raging	**4.** drip
2. rage	**5.** tune
3. dripping	**6.** tuneful

READING COMPREHENSION pages 185–186

UNDERSTANDING THE POEM
Possible answers:

1. The writer feels the winter months are cold, wet, and bleak.

2. The writer means that April does not have the winds of March, and in April the birds sing.

3. The month of June is sunny and brings the longest day.

4. August and September bring us corn and fruit.

5. The writer means that the leaves fall off the trees and plants in October.

6. Long nights and cold weather make December bleak.

FINDING THE MEANING OF THE POEM

Answers will vary.

Additional Reading Activity 1

See if students can identify the rhyming pattern by finding the rhyming words at the ends of the line of the poem.

Additional Reading Activity 2

Have students memorize lines from the poem so that they can recite them by heart. Give students lines about a month or a couple of months from the poem to memorize. Have students practice until they have remembered their lines perfectly. Then have a group that has memorized different months recite the poem to the class.

DISCUSSION page 186

Answers will vary.

CRITICAL THINKING page 186

Answers will vary.

WRITING ▪ 1

WRITING SKILLS pages 187–189

EXERCISE 1

January <u>cold</u> <u>desolate</u>;
February all <u>dripping</u> <u>wet</u>;
March wind rages;
April changes;
Birds sing in tune
To flowers of May,
And <u>sunny</u> June
Brings <u>longest</u> day;
In <u>scorched</u> July
The storm clouds fly
Lightning <u>torn</u>;
August bears corn,
September fruit;
In <u>rough</u> October
Earth must disrobe her;
Stars fall and shoot
In <u>keen</u> November;
And night is <u>long</u>
And cold is <u>strong</u>
In <u>bleak</u> December.

EXERCISE 2

Possible answers:

1. pretty
2. fierce
3. hot
4. lonely
5. longest
6. powerful
7. cloudy
8. colorful
9. large
10. distant

EXERCISE 3

A *Possible answers:*

Winter	Spring	Summer	Autumn
harsh	breezy	boiling	breezy
icy	cool	golden	cool
snowy	flowering	lazy	golden
	melting	sunburnt	
	new	breezy	
		harsh	

B *Answers will vary.*

EXERCISE 4

Answers will vary.

EXERCISE 5

Christina Rossetti **was** born in London, England in 1830. Her parents **were** from Naples, Italy. She **was** an **important** female writer of her time, and her writings are still popular today. After 1874, she **became** ill and rarely went out of her house. She **died** in 1894.

WRITING PRACTICE pages 189–190

Answers vary throughout this section.

JOURNAL

Ask students to write about the season that they like the most or the season that they like the least. Ask them to give good reasons for their like or dislike.

READING ■ 2
Fate

PRE-READING page 191

Begin the lesson in one of the following ways:

• Introduce the concepts of *folktale* and *fairy tale* to the class. Ask students to tell the class about any famous folktales or fairy tales from their culture or that they know of.

• Look at the title of the folktale "Fate." Make sure students understand the concept. Ask students if they believe in fate.

PREPARING FOR THE READING TOPIC

Answers will vary.

KEY VOCABULARY

1. b   3. a   5. c   7. d
2. g   4. e   6. h   8. f

VOCABULARY pages 194–195
VOCABULARY IN CONTEXT

A 1. stranger   5. fate
  2. journey   6. cured
  3. prepared   7. horrified
  4. refused   8. ill

B *Answers will vary.*

VOCABULARY BUILDING

1. cure   4. to prepare
2. to cure   5. horrific
3. preparation   6. horror

READING COMPREHENSION page 195
UNDERSTANDING THE FOLKTALE

Possible answers:

1. The prince asked the king for three bags of money to let him discover the world.

2. The prince learned his fate when a man in a palace showed him a piece of paper.

3. The weaver told the prince that he could give him the best they have.

4. The prince tried to kill the weaver's daughter so he might stop his fate.

5. The king was very happy.

6. The weaver's family bought a palace.

FINDING THE MEANING OF THE FOLKTALE

Answers will vary.

DISCUSSION page 196

Answers will vary.

CRITICAL THINKING page 196

Answers will vary.

WRITING ▪ 2

WRITING SKILLS pages 197–199

EXERCISE 1

There was once a <u>powerful</u> king, who had only one son, a prince. When the prince grew up, the king chose a princess for him to marry. The prince refused, saying, "It is not my fate to be with this girl. I will not marry her." Sometime later, the prince asked his father, "Will you please give me three bags of money and let me discover the world." The king agreed and gave him the money.

The prince set out on his journey. One day, he met a stranger, who asked, "Where are you going? What are you looking for?" The prince answered that he wanted to learn his fate. The stranger showed him a palace and said, "There you will learn your fate."

The prince went to the palace. Another man showed him a piece of paper with the words, *You will marry a weaver's daughter who has been <u>ill</u> for nine years.*

The prince was <u>horrified</u>. "I will change my fate," he said, and he left the palace. By evening, he was in a forest. He walked until he came to a <u>small</u> house. He asked to stay there for the <u>night</u>.

The man of the house replied, "Son, you are a <u>great</u> man. We have nothing for someone like you, but we can give you the best we have."

After supper, the prince noticed someone in another room. He asked who it was. His host answered, "I am a <u>poor</u> weaver, and I have only one daughter. She is <u>ill</u> and has been in bed for nine years."

When the prince heard this, he was <u>very</u> <u>surprised</u>. He didn't close his eyes that night. He was thinking of how he might stop his fate. In the middle of the night, he quietly entered the room of the weaver's daughter. He took out his dagger and pushed it into her. He went away and left his money behind him.

Years passed. One day the prince went out to hunt and saw a palace in the woods. In the palace was a <u>beautiful</u> <u>young</u> woman. He looked and looked at her. He thought he could look at her beauty forever. He went to her and asked her to marry him. She said yes.

The prince went home to tell his father that he was going to have a <u>beautiful</u> wife. The prince was <u>very</u> <u>happy</u>. The king was <u>happy</u>, too, and prepared a <u>big</u> wedding for his son.

Days after their marriage, the prince put his hand on his wife's heart. He felt something <u>hard</u> and asked, "What is this?"

His wife replied, "I am a <u>poor</u> weaver's daughter. For nine years I was <u>ill</u> in bed. One day a <u>young</u> man came to our house. He put his dagger into me and ran away. I was <u>very</u> <u>ill</u>, but my mother cured me. The <u>young</u> man left three bags of money. We bought a palace, my father gave up weaving, and we lived happily."

When the prince heard this, he said: "O God! Your words really are my fate!" Then he told his wife everything.

EXERCISE 2

Answers will vary.

EXERCISE 3

Answers will vary.

EXERCISE 4

Answers will vary.

EXERCISE 5

The old **q**ueen wanted to find out whether the girl was a real **p**rincess. So she **went** to the **bedroom,** took all the bedding off the bed**,** and put a pea on the bottom. Then**,** she took 20 mattresses and put **them** on top of **the** pea. Finally**,** she put 20 feather beds on top of the mattresses.

WRITING PRACTICE page 200

Answers vary throughout this section.

JOURNAL

Ask students to write about an event in their lives or in the life of someone they know that appears to have been fated.

WEAVING IT TOGETHER

TIMED WRITING page 201

Answers will vary.

SEARCH THE INTERNET page 201

A Suggested keywords:
   • a poem about love / nature / youth / old age

B Suggested keywords:
   • a folktale from [your country]

WHAT DO YOU THINK NOW? page 201

1. don't look
2. are
3. has
4. have

Notes

Notes

Notes

Notes